COUPLES MONEY

What Every Couple Should Know

about Money and Relationships

Marlow Felton

Chris Felton

"After reading this book, you will not look at
money or each other in the same way."
—Marlow and Chris Felton

ISBN: 1461148332
ISBN-13: 9781461148333
Library of Congress Control Number: 2011907129

Disclaimer:
This book does not make specific recommendations regarding investing or business ventures and does not intend to replace advice from a financial professional, tax professional, attorney, professional relationship counselor, or any other personalized professional advice.

Contents

Preface i

1. Our Stories 1

2. Identifying Money Personalities
   and Stories 7

3. Delusion 17

4. Unworthiness 25

5. Need for Approval 29

6. Financial Infidelity 33

7. Results and Prices 37

8. Projection and Resistance 41

9. Letting Go 51

10. Respecting Money 61

11. Segregating Funds: Theirs, Mine
    and Ours 65

12. Cash Flow 73

13. Making the Shift 81

14. Multiple Streams of Income:
    Being Entrepreneurial 89

15. Your Financial GPS System 97

16. Financial Intimacy 105

17. Being on the Same Page 109

18. Celebrate 117

19. A Couple Whose Dreams
    Came True 121

20. Summary of a Financially
    Harmonious Couple 125

COUPLES MONEY
Preface

The purpose of this book is to improve the quality of millions of relationships all over the world. After looking at numerous statistics, one can see that financial stress is a leading cause of divorce. In some studies, it ranked higher than infidelity. It is our desire to help other couples understand the complexities of what we call the "financial marriage" which can be more challenging than the physical marriage. We want to help couples work together to create a happy and successful financial relationship.

People place tremendous amounts of energy on money. When you combine two individuals with different ideas or relationships with money, the effects can weaken or even destroy the best relationships. We discuss the relationship with money and the relationship itself. Regardless of the type of relationship you are in, the concepts still apply. I hope many people read this book with their partner BEFORE they get married; however, it is never too late to learn and grow as a couple. We see numerous examples of couples who get married without any regard to each other's financial situation, habits or beliefs. It is analogous to buying a new home and ignoring the train tracks running through the open space behind the house. We see couples who don't even know what each other's goals and dreams are. Everyone has goals and dreams and they require money. Sharing these goals and dreams with a partner and working toward them together can create a lasting and fulfilling bond.

The examples outlined in this book come from our personal experiences as well as nineteen years of combined experience in the financial services industry, working with hundreds of couples from all walks of life. We also interviewed numerous couples with solid relationships who are financial independent. These couples' nest eggs are sufficient to sustain their current wants and needs for their combined lifetimes.

My husband and I were inspired to write this book as a result of our personal financial transformation and the financial struggles we have seen other couples experience nationwide. We are inspired by our mothers, Betty Felton and Patricia Ireland, who unfortunately both passed away from cancer. We saw them struggle in their relationships with financial issues and hope to inspire and help couples in their honor.

My husband and I went through a period when we felt stuck and frustrated. I was particularly frustrated and resented him for financial decisions he made that affected me. Everything came to a head one night, when I got so mad I started screaming at him and then threw my purse at him. I rattled off all the things I was angry about. I was tired and felt I deserved better and he was the cause! Then my husband said "Why are you married to me?" Great question. I had no immediate answer as I was reeling from anger; however, it forced me to think about why I was. This was the night that everything changed and I came to grips with my choices, not my husband's. The next day, with all the reasons I wanted to be married to my husband fresh in my head, we started a new chapter in our life together toward a happy financial marriage.

We both share our perspective throughout the chapters in this book. You will see "Her Perspective," which is mine, and "His Perspective", which is Chris's. There are also "action steps" at the end of each chapter. Don't feel that you have to do them all now. You can pick one from each chapter to do as you read and come back to do others later if you like.

1.
Our Stories

HER STORY

When I fell in love with Chris Felton, I never realized the implications of a "financial marriage". I fell in love with his personality, drive, our similar interests, and chemistry, of course. Most people do the same without considering the financial patterns and beliefs of their partner. Fortunately for us, we worked it out; however, many couples do not. I was married for the first time at age thirty-nine and had only been responsible for my finances. I had no idea what a "financial marriage" was or that it existed. I thought of it as a natural progression in a relationship that would eventually transpire.

My background was much different from Chris's and led me to different beliefs and patterns. Unlike Chris, I grew up in a household with no financial stress. I always knew we would take family trips every summer, presents would be under the tree at Christmas, clothes shopping would happen every season, etc., so I came to expect money. My dad was, however, very frugal, which became a negative experience with money for me. I found it embarrassing when we would dine out and my dad would leave a small tip. I decided I wasn't going to be cheap because I associated it with embarrassment. When I was out of college making my own financial decisions, I decided to be the opposite. I became a spender despite all the years of my dad telling me, "People with money have money because they're not throwing it away!" The fear of appearing cheap was stronger than the common sense that my dad attempted to teach me.

This pattern continued for years, and I ended up with a sobering amount of credit card debt. That was not the result I wanted; however, my underlying thought pattern around money led me there. I was scared straight and did a 180 to become a saver. I was determined to never have that happen again. This led me to the financial services industry. I was a sponge and wanted to learn everything there was to know about money and how it could work better for me. I started to get control of my finances as a young single woman of thirty-six. It never occurred to me at that point that I could lose the exciting feeling of financial control to my newfound "love of my life."

HIS STORY

Did you grow up in a household where financial stress was prevalent? My parents experienced financial stress. I watched them try to get ahead, make bad financial decisions, and eventually divorce over money issues. I watched them blame it on circumstances supposedly outside their control. From what I know now, they attracted and subconsciously created these situations.

When I was young, my dad told me I had to work hard. This message was confusing as both he and my mother worked very hard and never got ahead. They hardly saved and incurred debt just like many other American households. This financial reality was handed down to my siblings and me. So what did I do? I went to school, got good grades, borrowed the "hard work will make it all work" mentality, accomplished a few good things, and went into debt. I also thought that accumulating stuff and putting on a great show for approval of others was the key to happiness. I was doing everything that everyone else was doing and following the path everyone else was on— constantly working harder, attempting to prove my worth, and getting more into debt.

After financial struggles, challenges, starting my own business, a divorce, and a constant repetition of history, I knew I had to change. It really did not happen until I met an amazing woman, and coauthor of this book, Marlow. She had her own financial challenges as well, and the ironic part is we own a financial services business. We were instructing others what to do with their money and not following our own advice. I was spending, not saving, with debt increasing. I worked harder and harder, seventy to eighty hours per week, as the "hard work" program was always my answer. It seemed to only make the situation worse. The worst part was it was creating more stress in my second marriage.

Growing up, I also saw my mom stay in a relationship with my dad out of financial fear. The money she made would have been difficult for her to live on by herself, so she stayed in the relationship. I watched this weigh on my mom over the years as she was emotionally unfulfilled and felt trapped by her financial situation. Too often I see this pattern and hope to inspire other women or men to have the courage to change their financial situation and gain independence, or be able to work cohesively in their current relationship.

After talking to thousands of couples over the years regarding this topic, I have found the issues are similar. Unfortunately, most couples also associate with other couples with the same struggles and believe there is no other way. They have been handed beliefs about money from their parents that continue to repeat the unwanted reality.

The purpose of *Couples Money* is to share the story of what we did to turn our situation around as well as provide insights from other couples who have overcome financial struggles. Our deepest purpose for writing this book is to give you the belief that you can change so your marriage and family can prosper and future generations do not have to continue along the same path.

Action Steps:

1. *Think back to your early experiences with money. What did you learn from these, and how are these experiences influencing your views about money? Where do you see this impacting your life?*

2. *Discuss this with your partner and share how these early memories shaped your perceptions of money.*

2.

Identifying Money Personalities and Stories

HER PERSPECTIVE

We all have money stories we tell ourselves over and over that create our financial reality, so our current financial situation is nothing more than a story we made up and believe. We learn most of these stories as children when we are developing ideas about ourselves and the world around us. How can siblings grow up in the same environment and turn out with such different lives? It is because they made up different stories based on his or her perception of an experience. Think about two people looking at an abstract painting and being asked what they see. Usually, you get two different answers. The same happens with our money stories and our interpretation of money.

I have met many couples who grew up in similar households, yet created different outcomes in their financial lives. They can grow up in a household where there was plenty of money; however, one learned to believe that money is evil because of being teased at school. This person decided money must be bad because it causes people to dislike you, and this belief is bound to subconsciously affect his financial results. It keeps him from going after a higher-paying job or causes him to sabotage financial success with overspending.

My husband and I spent many hours talking about our financial beliefs based on early experiences with money. This is a great exercise for any couple to go through. If you recall something that happened twenty-five years ago or more, you remember that event for a significant reason. Think about how you felt and what belief you created as a result. Then ask yourself if that belief is serving you today. If it is not, talk with your partner about ways you can consciously choose to do the opposite. Start to tell yourself a different story. You chose your money story in the first place, so you can create a new one, too. In the example above, believing that money is evil, choose to act differently when an opportunity to make money presents itself, or when you overspend out of habit. Your partner can help you see when you may be reverting back to your old story.

We also have a money personality. I shared my story earlier about being a spender and then becoming a saver. The good news is these personalities do not need to be permanent. Don't label yourself by your current reality if that is not what you want. These personalities are helpful for you to understand you and your partner's core beliefs about money, so it is critical to address in order to develop a plan for financial harmony.

There are four basic personalities I will share with you and discuss their tendencies toward money. I first learned of these personalities through PSI Seminars[1] and have applied them specifically to money. There are no hard and fast rules, and many people have a combination of all four. Usually, however, one of them is the most dominant. Within these four styles people can be a "spender," a "saver," or an "avoider."

The Controller: Controllers like to be in control; they like to be right and tend to be structured in their activities. They plan everything and are not naturally spontaneous. They can have huge egos that may cause them to be spenders in order to look good and hold up the image of having it all together. They can be good savers when they want to be since they like the idea of a budget and can usually stick to it because they crave structure. They tend to be CEOs of companies, managers, like to be in charge and are usually not avoiders since they are hands-on, take-charge people. Controllers in a relationship need to be involved in the day-to-day finances and may be best suited to take care of the bill paying, etc. Two controllers are probably happier when managing them together. I know this personality well because I am one of them! When my husband and I first were married, he handled the household finances and his finances while I managed mine. My husband thought he was doing me a favor by handling this tedious task when it was actually driving me crazy not to be in control of all the details. My husband now believes that handing over the finances to me was one of the best decisions he made. We still, however, go over our finances regularly.

The Promoter: Promoters love to be liked! They are usually popular and the life of the party. Having fun is important to them, and they love being the center of attention and usually are. They are great sales people, entertainers, charismatic leaders, and great public speakers. They can spend money like crazy for the sake of a good time. They dislike structure, so controllers watch out! They can be avoiders when the thrill of the moment hits them, and they throw the budget out the window. They are motivated to save when they see a purpose to save. When partnered with a promoter, you can be the most successful in motivating them to stick to a budget by showing them how it will create more money for the dream retirement or saving to buy a new house (where they can have friends over). My husband is a promoter, but luckily has enough of the other three personalities and common sense to balance things out. His promoter characteristics are useful in our business where I utilize them all the time and he is also a lot of fun to be around.

The Supporter: Supporters are caring and loving people. They love to help people, and family is important to them. They often are nurses, firemen, teachers, work for nonprofits, etc. They can be good savers when focused on financial stability for their family but can be great avoiders of financial issues with the excuse "it's not their thing." A supporter who is an avoider can best be motivated to pay attention to the finances when it relates to the family or helping others. They can be spenders when avoiding financial structure and focusing on taking care of others. They are generally not structured and tend to dislike a budget unless they see how it might help their family or others close to them. They can also give all their money away taking care of other people. If your partner is a supporter and you are not, you need to be patient with her. If you explain how you feel about your finances and how important her role is to you, you will get much further than getting frustrated. Explain your goals and dreams and encourage her to share hers and then offer to put a mutual plan together to build your dreams. Supporters really want love, so anything that sounds like more love will move them.

The Analyst: Analysts fear being wrong or making a wrong decision. They research everything before they act, and this can be frustrating for a promoter, who makes quick decisions. They like data and crave structure. Accountants, engineers, and airline pilots are usually analysts. They are usually good savers and love budgets, but can be overly conservative with their money out of fear of doing the wrong thing. They can be avoiders of financial results by hiding behind data and fancy spreadsheets and can be great at creating delusion. They can suffer from "paralysis by analysis," and their inability to act quickly to an opportunity can cause negative financial results. The best way to motivate analysts is to show them facts and data. Show them the facts and figures of a good decision and focus on that, but be careful not to show them too much, as they can get caught up in the details. They are logic driven, so simple matter-of-fact statements are good. They want to be involved in the day-to-day finances and may prefer to do most of it—just ensure that there is a regularly scheduled progress meeting. They might create spreadsheets and graphs that you can ooh and aah over.

Any of these four money personalities can be "avoiders" although I have found most avoiders tend to be supporters and promoters. "Avoiders" avoid conversations about money at all cost and do not like thinking about money or being responsible for keeping track of it. They often say, "It's just not my thing," and let others handle the money, or they handle it with devastating results. The irony here is that avoiders also have goals and dreams that cost money; however, they don't make the connection to their avoidance and unrealized goals and dreams because they are so far in denial. They associate money and keeping track of their money with requiring superior math, investment, or fancy spreadsheet skills. My advice to avoiders is to have someone else take care of the financial details they don't like, but it is still critical to be engaged, aware, and accountable for their goals and dreams to be realized.

We talk quite a bit about "spenders" and "savers." Most people have a tendency toward one or the other, based on childhood experiences that shaped their beliefs. Some people become savers if their parents saved money while others become spenders based on their parents being savers. This can happen for a variety of reasons, mainly our interpretation of the experience. I became a spender, as I associated embarrassment with saving money. I thought my dad was overly frugal and cheap, which was embarrassing to me. I decided I didn't want that, so I created a story that spending was better. When I realized it, I consciously changed my story because I realized my goals and dreams were more important than how people might perceive me. I told myself I was a great saver because that would give me the results I wanted. "Spender" and "saver" can be temporary labels you ultimately choose.

Think about your spending and saving habits based on results. Please don't fool yourself that you are a "saver" if you have little money saved. The proof is in the results. You know you are a "spender" if: You have mentally spent your paycheck before it even comes. You rationalize the purchase on sale as "saving" money when the truth is, you will just spend it on something else. You have not "saved" any money unless it has actually been deposited into your account. Spenders blow money without regard to consequences, and when they run out of money, they scramble to create more. Some people are successful doing this and therefore keep repeating the behavior. They fool themselves by thinking they will always be able to make more money. Many men tend to have this characteristic, and it can be stressful and detrimental to a relationship where the partner craves structure and security.

The concept of saving money may scare some and sound elementary to others. There are varying degrees of saving, and some people are fooled into thinking they are good savers. People tell me they are good at shopping for bargains and "saving" money. So where is it? They have little or no money saved. The beauty of "saving" money is actually "saving" the money. If my husband and I found an area of excessive spending, we increased an investment auto-deduct by the same amount. For example, we lowered our cell phone bill by $50 a month and increased our automatic savings by $50 a month. This may sound simple, but most people don't do this in reality. Partners should hold each other accountable in this area.

"Savers" save at least 10 percent of their income on a regular basis, no exceptions, and it is accumulating (meaning they are not dipping in to it!). They have a comfortable cushion for short-term expenses and still have other savings. They also have no credit card debt. They actually enjoy saving money! Yes, "spenders," it can be fun and rewarding. A financially independent couple I know told me saving is fun for them. They have savings goals they have agreed on and remind each other often. Once they started to see the money accumulate and their new habits created new results, they became addicted to saving. The new habits they formed became permanent and have allowed them to hold onto their wealth. It was important for them to keep the same habits that got them to financial independence to keep them there.

It was interesting for me to discover that quite a few financially independent people refer to themselves as "spenders." Is this because they have quite a bit of money to spend? They may be spending money; however, I also found they have a structured plan around saving, and spend only what is left over. They create assets that spin off sufficient cash flow that is used for spending. Savers determine what they want and then create the plan to pay for it.

HIS PERSPECTIVE

Ditto. My Controller wife is always right. She happy, me happy!

Action Steps:

1. *Talk to your partner about your perceived money personality and how you perceive his or her money personality.*

2. *Discuss how you can better communicate with your partner with his or her money personality in mind.*

3.
Delusion

Couples can keep each other delusional. Making money vs. keeping money. I have watched numerous couples make a lot of money and not keep any of it. They are counting on their income to continue. This is a form of self-sabotage and delusion. Many couples who own businesses fall into the "I'm putting it back into the business" or "It's a business expense" trap. They use that as an excuse not to save money that will work for them regardless of what their business does. They both have used this so many times that they have each other believing it is what they should do.

Financially independent couples stayed that way because they do not let each other fall into the trap of delusion and justifying expenses. They know an expense is still an expense that keeps money from working for them and treat their business as a stream of income that could be temporary. They know there is no guarantee the income will continue or that they will be able to sell their business for a profit. They carefully consider their return on investment before acting.

Couples seem to feed off each other's bad money habits and perpetuate a downward spiral. Together, a couple's bad money habits are easily doubled. Have you ever bought something just because your partner did? If he or she is going to have something, you should have it too. You took one bad financial decision and doubled it. The good news is when a couple decides they want to change, those efforts can be doubled as well. They can even make quantum leaps together when on the same page.

I worked with a couple who told me they weren't sure where their money was going. After creating a detailed budget they discovered they were taking out $20 in cash from the ATM almost unconsciously. This seemingly harmless act was totaling $800/month. The problem was that there was no accountability for the action and they had both succumbed to the idea that they just didn't have any money to save. They were keeping each other in the delusion that $20 here and there out of the ATM was not a problem, but they soon realized that having $800 a month to save was more significant.

HIS PERSPECTIVE

Have you ever felt financially stuck? Are you there now? When someone gets stuck, they are usually resisting where they are. They tell themselves that everything is fine or that everything will get better when something specific happens. They might be counting on a big sale to make everything work out or the "big deal" to come through. They are masters of delusion, usually avoid money conversations, and maybe even balancing their checkbook. The "avoider" personality types are masters of delusion who put up a good front to keep them and loved ones happy. They refuse to look at the hard facts in relation to their financial situation and are great at making up excuses for not taking care of things and for the situation. They are usually "VERY BUSY!" or say "My husband/wife spends too much money," "My boss didn't give me a raise," and my favorite "The economy is bad." The list can go on and on. This is called resisting what is, or not accepting circumstances as they are. They lack personal responsibility. Delusion is also caused by a "victim" mentality, which means believing your financial well-being has something to do with circumstances outside your control. Delusion lays the responsibility on something or someone else.

I have found that people in general are delusional around money and have the habit of associating with others with the same characteristics. Your associations are very powerful as they shape how you think and act, especially when it comes to money and finance. These associations can support these beliefs and further the delusion. Couples and family members are the most powerful associations, and if not truthful about their financial situation, they will perpetuate the delusion, as it helps them justify where they are. An example of this would be seeing a close friend or relative buy a new car. You have no idea if this is a sound financial decision on his or her part because you don't have all the information; however, you feel as if it is now okay for you to buy a new car.

Delusion is a symptom; the key is to find the root. When looking at the symptom vs. the root of any problem, the root is usually created by stories that go unchecked through most people's lives. We have been telling ourselves the same stories for so long, most people don't even know where they learned these beliefs. Unworthiness or not deserving exists in a large percentage of the world's population and therefore leads to delusional thought processes, such as "you are either rich or you're not," "money is the root of all evil," etc. When people do not take a look at these beliefs, delusion and denial run them.

Most people are attached to false stories and assumptions that they came to believe as children. It is unhealthy how we buy a story, let it run unconsciously, and believe that we cannot make a change. Look at the financial results you have in your life and your relationship. This is a result of what you subconsciously believe to be true because of something you learned a long time ago. For example, if someone was told as a child "rich people are crooks" and she believed it, she would grow up with that subconsciously playing in her head and creating a seemingly undesirable financial reality. She could have seen her parents fight about money and subconsciously believe that money causes problems, so she doesn't make much money (which we know can cause other problems). To break this cycle, we have to recognize the undesirable result, discover the root story we have been telling ourselves, and then consciously decide to tell ourselves a new story over and over. This requires discipline, repetition, reinforcement from ourselves and a partner, and is powerful.

The delusion stems from looking at something neutral, such as money, through what I would call "the wrong set of lenses." If you see the eye doctor and he updates your prescription with a sharper lens, the difference in clarity is substantial. Something before might have looked blurry and confusing until you put on a better lens and are able to look at the true picture. Money perception is similar, and the purpose of changing your beliefs about money to something more positive is to give you better vision and perception to one of the most crucial elements of your life.

The way to stay delusional and in denial is not to take responsibility for your financial results. This is being totally unclear about your present situation. If you are not willing to know or look, you will continue the delusional behavior. My favorite crutch in the past was denial. I wanted to remain positive and tried to sell "everything was going to work out" to my wife. This is a great way to stay positive, but if never looking at where you are and not getting clear about where you are going, your positivity becomes a delusion and you are only dreaming. My other favorite story I was telling myself was "I know I will be successful one day," but that day was continuing to be pushed off and was never to be obtained until I dealt with reality. Change occurs when you accept reality, stop beating yourself up, and start moving. Unfortunately, couples with the same delusional tendencies feed off each other, and negative energy continues to perpetuate the issues. Two people feeding off each other's delusion can have exponential results. People would rather talk about anything than their financial reality, as they feel the personal hit for being where they are. People's need to be right is powerful, so it is easier to be delusional than to accept that their money behavior is "not right" or take responsibility for their role in their financial reality.

I know this one well, as my background would appear to equate to financial success. Being a good student, I graduated cum laude from my university. I was a CPA with a Big-Six public accounting firm and running a successful financial services firm. It was easier to be delusional than to look at my behavior. We were making great money by most people's standards, but it was vanishing as quickly as it came in. For me to be wrong would have impacted this lofty image. It was easier to put up appearances, tell myself lies, and justify to Marlow that everything was okay. Delusion was a way of life, but it almost cost me everything. This perpetual, ego-driven behavior keeps people stuck in delusion. It is like a four-thousand-pound elephant in the room that no one wants to talk about, and many couples can ignore it for years as it erodes at their relationship.

Wealth is created from the inside out, which includes realizing delusional tendencies and addressing them even if it is uncomfortable. You know if you are in delusion if you are clueless about where you are and unwilling to deal with it. What you ignore persists. Look at any undesirable financial results you may have in your life and know that there is an unrealized root cause or one that is being ignored. The best way to uncover these root causes is to ask a series of questions, including the following: What am I trying to achieve? What am I trying to avoid? What are the stories I am telling myself about money? Where did I first learn this story? Is it even true? Is it serving me?

I have seen a lot of people in dire financial circumstances who feel they can fix themselves. They are unwilling to solicit help, as they let their ego get in the way and don't want to look clueless or be vulnerable. Getting free financially and breaking from delusion is a team sport, and I believe couples need to solicit help from the right associations and get coaching and feedback to break from this destructive thought process. Get with a trusted advisor or financially successful friend and ask him or her to give you feedback on how you are around money. Feedback is powerful, yet most people never ask for it. I have found the growth from feedback can be life changing. If you are clear on the results you want, you will seek it as a huge motive to change. I also recommend hiring a personal coach for you and your partner, as I did, who will hold you accountable on your desired areas of change.

Action Steps:

1. *Find someone trusted, more financially successful than yourself who will give you honest feedback and hold you accountable.*

2. *Make a list of your associations, friends, family, etc. Are their beliefs about money positive or negative? How has this affected your beliefs? How can you improve your associations to include people with positive beliefs about money?*

4.
Unworthiness

HER PERSPECTIVE

I often meet with clients that have an underlying thought process of unworthiness. Most don't even realize they feel unworthy of wealth in their life; however, the proof is in the lack of wealth in their life. It is one of the most destructive beliefs anyone can have and causes people to under earn their potential and sabotage wealth when it comes to them. I am grateful that I have always believed I deserved to be wealthy.

HIS PERSPECTIVE

Our persistent thoughts, whether good or bad, create the greatest consequences of our lives. We often think things need to change outside of us; however, change occurs on the inside first. You must be aware of your negative self-talk. If in a negative state, your internal feeling is negative, and it affects how you feel. One of the most destructive negative thoughts relates to unworthiness, not deserving or feeling not good enough. This is one of the major causes of pain and destructive behavior around money. Judging yourself as undeserving is poisonous to your energy and your goals, and the biggest root of self-sabotage. You will never out earn your self-image.

When growing up we heard more noes than yeses and were punished for being wrong by our teachers, parents, and those around us. We were conditioned, and as we grew up, we started implementing the punishment ourselves. It all became a story we felt obligated to believe. When we believe we are not good enough, we unconsciously attract the financial situations to prove we are right. We all like to be right, don't we? We do this over and over, and it sticks like a broken record. Wealthy people collect evidence to support their success; unworthy people do the opposite. The good news is that our story can be changed; the potential bad news for some is it takes work.

One place to start is by writing down the image of the person you want to become. Be very detailed and use other successful people as an example. How would totally deserving people act, behave, or talk to themselves? How would they interact with others? In talking with successful people, I have found that many were not born with a great self-image, and many had significant limiting beliefs about themselves. Once they got clear on what they wanted and it became emotional, they consciously decided not to allow that negative self-image to hold them back. They created an image of their life and who they wanted to become, they contemplated, meditated, visualized, and studied until they became the image. They knew they would have to force themselves to remember this ideal image over and over until it became part of them.

What are the prices that you and your loved ones are paying for your feeling of unworthiness? Once you connect the dots, you will want to go to work on this immediately. Alter your self-talk by telling yourself frequently you deserve it and that you are capable of making it happen. When a negative thought occurs, reverse it with positive self-talk. Accept yourself for who you are, focus on the great things about you, and FORGIVE yourself. Get the picture of who you want to become, make the changes, gather support, move in the direction, and enjoy the journey. Growth is necessary, but it is impossible to move forward in a state of negativity and continued devaluation of you. You have talents and gifts totally unique to you, and you must remind yourself of them constantly. Have fun with it, celebrate your accomplishments, and frequently tell yourself you do DESERVE success and wealth.

Action Step:

1. *Tell yourself "I deserve to be wealthy," continuously.*

2. *Tell your partner he or she deserves to be wealthy.*

3. *Write down in detail the person you want to become. Spend five minutes a day visualizing yourself as this person.*

5.
Need for Approval

You have more than likely heard the phrase "Keeping up with the Joneses"? Well, I've met the proverbial Joneses, and they are broke because they are trying to keep up with you. People do a great job keeping up the façade, as they perpetuate the emotional need to compete materialistically with each other. The Joneses wouldn't like their friends to see their credit card statements and retirement accounts. This may sound harsh; however, after meeting with hundreds of couples, I no longer look at the guy next to me in traffic in the nice car or the lady with the expensive outfit the same. I know in many cases this purchase was not a sound financial decision because I have met with couple after couple where this was the case.

It takes one to know one, of course, and my "look good" program is pretty strong. This has been helpful in keeping me in shape, because being overweight would not serve this "look good" program. I work out regularly and am the lady who puts on mascara and eyeliner to go to the gym.

This same need to look good, however, has its pitfalls. As I have already discussed, I was quite the spender at one time. What did I spend money on? Mainly items that would make me look good, of course. I was a victim of the "Keep up with the Joneses" mentality until I realized it was not getting me where I wanted to be—financial independence.

HIS PERSPECTIVE

I have a successful friend, Joe Gregory, a sales trainer who often states to his clients, "your need for approval is the biggest check you will ever write." Worrying about what others think or how we look stops us from taking steps toward financial independence. This can result in negative financial results. This can be applied to any instance in your life, but is really relevant with money and finance. How do I know? My need for approval has unconsciously controlled me for most of my life. I realized all of my good and bad financial decisions were the result of this need for approval from others. It caused me to be an athletic over achiever when I was young to get approval from my peers. In college, it was the basis of academic success that led to a successful career. I was always searching for the approval of others.

Seeking approval can have positive results, yet the negative consequences can have a hefty price tag. I needed to look good to others, so I bought a house I could not afford, drove an expensive car that was unnecessary, and always picked up the tab. It was unconscious and led to money flowing out at an aggressive rate, massive debt, and stress on me and Marlow. I recognized some startling revelations. One, you will never get the approval of everyone, so you might as well stop now. I had to be good with me and internally at peace instead of searching for external things to complete me. You may have heard the saying "Often fed, never satisfied." This was me, because once I won the approval, I was out searching for it again. This hurt my first marriage and was beginning to impact this one.

People, spend, drink, and eat, etc., to fill these voids. I filled the void with overworking, spending, and seeking others to prove myself to. I was on the "layaway plan" of life, stating to myself, one day I will be happy and fulfilled. This was the root to most of my bad financial decisions. It was not until I fully accepted myself for who I was with both the good and the bad that it was cured. The need for approval still resides, but I am now aware when it surfaces. When this old dysfunctional friend comes back, I am aware and consciously choose to stop the behavior.

I constantly see approval issues in people. They develop an armor to create the appearance that things are great. My armor was homes and cars, even though I was internally miserable. I finally realized that I could choose happiness now, love myself now, and be in integrity with myself. The results improved dramatically. The recent recession showed who was real and who was not. We are not our homes, our cars, or our stuff. The quicker you detach your identity from those items and attach it to making yourself whole, the sooner you can forge your path to true happiness and financial freedom.

5. Need for Approval

Action Steps:

1. *Write down financial decisions you have made in order to seek approval.*

2. *Think about how this is affecting your life right now.*

6.
Financial Infidelity

People place significant emotion on money. Money can bring much pleasure or much pain. It can signify power, freedom, independence, and happiness. Knowing this, our habits and behavior around money have a significant impact on our relationships, and most are unaware. We can do things that emotionally betray our partner financially and can be as devastating as an affair. I see the looks on people's faces when they tell me about their partner's credit card debt or the motorcycle they bought without discussing it first. It is a look of hurt and betrayal that can be difficult to mend. This can go on for years and silently chips away at the relationship. I know a couple that divorced after forty years of marriage because of the husband's financial irresponsibility and lack of accountability to the spouse. It finally became too much, and they separated. This is financial infidelity.

Financial infidelity isn't always the large purchases or the big financial mistakes. It can be little, seemingly insignificant acts that add up over time. Have you ever hid a new purchase in the trunk of your car until you could get it safely into the house without your partner seeing? Have you ever lied about how much something cost so your partner wouldn't get upset? Not being honest about money, no matter how small, chisels away at trust in a marriage similar to infidelity. We put as much emotional energy on money as we do sex. Finding out your partner did something they know the other would not agree to, is a disappointing blow.

Another form of financial infidelity is revenge spending, and I did it. We were in Hawaii one year, and my husband golfed every day. Did he expect me to sit quietly by the pool reading my book? How much was he spending anyway? We had never discussed that, of course. I got mad and was going to get even. Or so I thought. I went to the spa and racked up a $1,000 bill. That will show him. It certainly showed him how expensive a massage, facial, and a mud wrap can be. We both ended up paying the price for that emotionally and financially.

Revenge spending becomes a game of financial tug of war. I know couples who have revenge spent themselves into huge amounts of credit card debt without even realizing what they were doing. First, it was his flat screen TV, then her new purse, and then his trip to Las Vegas with his buddies. Where will it end? Bankruptcy? Did this couple intend on bankruptcy? Of course not, but that is where they ended up because they let emotions take control. Then, tragically, they lost sight of their goals and dreams.

Any type of financial infidelity can destroy even the best relationships, silently building resentment between two people. I got so mad at my husband that it didn't occur to me to have an adult conversation with him about how I felt. My emotions were high and blocked logic. He never asked me about why I spent all that money in the spa, so this, in turn, made it okay for him to spend more money without discussing it with me. I grew angrier at him, and the resentment kept brewing.

Unfortunately, this lingered for some time until I blew up. We were then forced to have the conversations we should have had along the way. Don't think feelings of resentment or anger will just go away. They are signs that something must be dealt with. The sooner you deal with it the better, as in the example of the couple that divorced after forty years. They spent forty years of their lives feeling this way, when they really loved each other, but unfortunately let forty years of financial infidelity escalate to an unbearable level.

HIS PERSPECTIVE

My form of financial infidelity was to think I could spend the money I made however I wanted and never made the connection to our goals and dreams. It was selfish, self-righteous, and destructive with the results to prove it. I justified the spending and never communicated the results until Marlow took over the finances. The accountability was there, and I had to think twice before making a financial decision that was not in our collective best interest.

The big move was making the mental change from my money to our money. What I spent was not just impacting me—it was affecting us. Realizing the emotional impact began to override some old, bad spending habits. I previously thought spending "my" money was no big deal, but these negative thoughts and selfishness began to seep into other areas of our relationship in a negative way.

Action Steps:

1. *Answer these questions:*

   How have you been financially unfaithful to your partner? Does your partner know about it? How has this impacted your relationship? How has that impacted your financial situation?

7.

Results and Prices

HER PERSPECTIVE

When we were at the lowest point, my overriding feeling was resentment—resentment for the choices my husband made that affected me. This made me angry (thus the purse throwing incident). I went months without communicating this to Chris, and it consumed me. This caused a great deal of stress, which negatively impacted every other area of my life: my career, my health, our financial life, and my relationship with Chris. I was wasting time feeling resentful when I should have focused on a solution, and this cost us about three years of time off our current financial plan. I am grateful that I realized the price I was paying and chose to deal with my reality.

HIS PERSPECTIVE

During our period of financial stress, I was in denial. I was great at looking ahead but not knowing where we were. By not knowing where we were, my decision making stayed the same. The "one day it will get better" mentality caused me to spend rather than budget and make the necessary changes, as I deluded myself into believing I could continue to spend because "one day it will get better." I am not saying that optimism is not a good thing, but if you are feeling stuck and continuing to deny it, you will remain stuck. You can be positive about where you are going and still not move. It is difficult to move forward without taking a hard look at your current reality.

Planning a trip anywhere, you have a start point (point A) and an end point (point B). Most do not know or want to look at their current financial condition (point A). Ego plays a big part in this and is a powerful force that keeps people from admitting they need to change. Ego can also keep you from taking responsibility. This also leads to laying blame, justification, or excuses, which keep you stuck and believing that you are powerless to change.

That was me. I was allowing my ego and my need to be right to run my financial life. I had numerous built-in "victim" excuses that also did not serve me. Once I figured out the common denominator with the issue was me and accepted that, I was able to stop, look at the results, where we were, and the prices others were paying, in order for change to occur. The major impetus for change was the price that my wife was paying. The financial stress was impacting her happiness, health, career, and worse, our marriage. When I connected how I was behaving around money and the pain my delusional behavior was causing Marlow, I knew I had to change.

Further prices related to spending time with my kids, other relationships, lack of happiness in my life, and also my lack of integrity around teaching others how to plan financially but not following through on my own plan. It impacted my energy, my business leadership role, my health, etc. These prices were heavy, and I knew it would get worse unless I changed.

The major paradox around change is that people expect circumstances outside of them to change but insist on staying the same. I realized that change had to happen internally before external circumstances between my wife and me could improve. Saving money always made sense to me, and I had all the knowledge and tools to know what to do with money, but based on results, this logic was not getting it done. Only when I connected emotional reasons to saving money (Marlow's happiness, our marriage working, time with my kids) was I able to shift and override my ego, my need for approval from others, my need to look good, and my need to be right. By connecting these prices with my actions and results, it became emotional. We are all emotional creatures, and change can only work if compelling emotional reasons are applied.

The positive emotional needs began to consume my thinking as I dreamt of the feeling of relief, happiness, and accomplishment once I changed and we hit our financial goals. As the positive emotion took over, action and changes began to occur. Denial was replaced with a real vision, and most importantly, the focused goal of saving money was tied back to positive, emotional, compelling reasons.

People create change when great pain is presented, but waiting for this triggering event is unnecessary. Don't beat yourself up, make yourself wrong, or create a bigger problem. You may not like where you are, but put yourself in the mindset of where you want to go. Forgive yourself, accept your reality, and create solutions to move.

Action Steps:

1. Determine your point A and write it down in detail.

2. Write down the prices being paid by your loved ones as a result of your point A.

3. Forgive yourself and your partner. Exchange vows: "Even though we are _____, I accept myself and you fully and completely."

8.
Projection and Resistance

HER PERSPECTIVE

Sometimes the harder you try to get unstuck, the worse things get. This is being in resistance to "what is" or denial of something. If you feel stuck and frustrated, there is something dragging you down that you haven't dealt with. It is like trying to run a marathon with an anchor tied to your ankle. Resistance takes on many forms, and the first step to changing your financial reality is to let go of these anchors. Easier said than done, especially if you don't know what that is.

Finding out what is dragging you down may take some time and serious introspection. The following helped me release an anchor that was holding me back. Think about all the things your partner does with money that annoys you, makes you angry, or you don't like. Also, think about some things other people around you do with money that annoys or angers you. Take a few minutes to write these down.

The things that you noted are what keep you stuck. You cannot have a negative thought about someone else without seeing the same tendency in yourself. Negative thoughts around people are really more about us than them. They are emotional anchors that keep prosperity away. Financial problems are a result of something you do not want to accept about yourself that you keep trying to repress. This is known as resistance to "what is," and the harder we try to fight it, the less likely we are to be open to solutions to move us away from an undesirable financial situation. I created an undesirable reality because I was unwilling to accept my financial reality and take responsibility for what I had done in the past. This came out in the form of resentment and anger toward my husband and kept me from seeing possible solutions because I was caught up in my anger toward him, not realizing where it was coming from.

When I felt resentment toward my husband, I was really projecting dislike of my past behavior. I had a history of overspending and debt, and it scared me to see things snowball like they had, so I was determined never to be there again. I did a 180 and was saving money and feeling pretty good. It didn't occur to me when we got married that we were not on the same page. When I realized where he was financially and saw his patterns of spending, it scared me. I wasn't sure what to do, and I didn't talk to him about it. Instead, I let my fear get the best of me.

I realized some huge lessons the night I blew up at him and threw my purse. First, I had to take responsibility for my choices. I was the one who chose to marry my husband, and if I didn't want to stay married to him, I certainly didn't need to. I thought about what I would have to give up if I chose not to stay married to him. I discovered I was unwilling to be without all his other wonderful qualities. The second lesson was that I had to be part of the solution and work through it with him. By changing my focus on the reasons I wanted to stay married to Chris, and taking responsibility, I let go of my resentment little by little, and slowly things started to change. Looking back, the moment I began to appreciate my husband more, I began to let go of my anger. By taking responsibility for my actions, I felt more in control of my future actions and results. If I was responsible for the choices that created the undesirable results, I could also be responsible for new choices that could create positive results. When I realized this, significant changes started to happen. Most importantly, we worked on it together and got on the same page.

Projection can take on many forms. Sometimes our desire NOT to be something can be more powerful than our desire to BE something. This can be a result of negative childhood memories. As previously mentioned, my father was overly frugal and embarrassingly cheap in my mind. I did not want to be this way, so I became "programmed" to spend money as a way to avoid being perceived as cheap. If I had written down a list of things that other people did that annoyed me fifteen years ago, being cheap would have been at the top of the list. I am now aware that I was trying to avoid being cheap and realize the results I created through avoidance are not what I want. Now, very little emotion pops up for me if I see that in someone. I rarely even think about it.

I know a lady who was an only child. Growing up, she was constantly told she was spoiled. She disliked being told this and decided unconsciously as a child that she did not want to be spoiled, nor did she want anyone to think she was spoiled. What did she do? She gave every extra dime from her business away. She didn't charge what she was worth so she wouldn't have to worry about making too much money. She was successful at never saving any money or creating financial stability for her family. Her relationships paid the ultimate price as a result. She wondered for years why she wasn't able to get ahead because she was doing this unconsciously. It was only when she sat down and made a list of characteristics of other people that drove her crazy that she realized this. "Spoiled" was at the top of her list. She thought about how she felt when people called her spoiled and realized the pattern she had created. She also saw the prices she and her family were paying, and things began to change.

How far are you willing to go to prove you are not those items you listed earlier? Get into debt to prove you aren't poor; avoid making money so you don't come across as "better than." Have you ever tried to hold a beach ball under the water? It doesn't last long, does it? We try so hard to bury those characteristics we do not like in ourselves; however, that will only work for so long. Eventually it will pop up. Resistance to "what is" pops up in the form of bankruptcy, foreclosure, ruined relationships, and dreams unrealized. It pops up in our relationships and can destroy them. I know couples where one criticized the other and held resentment over the other's spending, only to get caught making a huge purchase or financial mistake behind the other's back.

When you experience anger, resentment, or fear, it is a sign you are projecting and in resistance to something you perceive as negative. When we experience these feelings, are we any fun? Do you think people want to help or conduct business with someone like that? This is how projection keeps money from us. Resistance to what is takes a lot of energy and leaves us exhausted. This is energy that could be used to move us forward, but instead is holding us back. Our partners, being the closest to us, become the natural targets for our projections. It is so easy to get mad, resentful, and angry at them when we are really mad at ourselves. This perpetuates the downward spiral without us realizing what we are doing. It is counterproductive and creates a volatile situation for a couple.

HIS PERSPECTIVE

People spend most of their lives in resistance, meaning living in fear, worry, doubt, anger, resentment, attached to negativity, etc. Awareness is the key when you are in resistance or attached to situations, circumstances, and negative thoughts. I often know I am in resistance by how I feel. When I feel frustrated, angry, resentful, or otherwise negative, I know I am in resistance. I must move into a better feeling (enthusiasm or positivity) to improve my results. Surrendering these feelings of resistance is necessary to achieving your financial goals and learning to let go is a lifelong process.

Anytime we allow outside circumstances to impact how we feel, we are giving away our power and cannot create solutions to move forward. Allowing these feelings to control you stops your progress, drains your energy, and further creates counterproductive results. I have used techniques such as journaling, meditation, breathing, affirmations, and visualization to shift out of resistance and away from my negative feelings. The majority of people have resistance to money, debt, etc. They think about the debt, lack of money, etc., and feel negative emotions around their current reality.

What you resist persists. For example, if you continue to be in debt, there is no secret to why; you just need to figure out what you are resisting. Write down all the things in your financial life that you wish would change. These can be financial situations or circumstances you are angry about that cause fear, doubt, or other negativity. Take your time and create a thorough list. Write down your feelings about each one. These are the things you resist. If I ask you how you are going to make the changes to create a different result, most would say, "I will fix it," which is what they have been attempting to do. The list for me was related to debt and struggling financially. I had tremendous resistance to those things. I thought I would fix them, but I continued to try and nothing was changing. The lesson is this. People attempt to change while in resistance, and it DOES NOT WORK. Until my attitude about those things changed, nothing would ever change. I had to accept the reality, take responsibility, and stop beating myself up about my results. This does not mean that I liked it or that I gave up, but I had to shift from negative thoughts on my list for anything to change. It took some work, but all those negative items were handled. I accepted, got into a mastermind with Marlow, my coach, and others, and created solutions for changing me and our situation. I was the common denominator to all those items, and they would not change until I did.

The way to stay in resistance is to keep telling your story as it is (point A) vs. how you want it to be (point B). I knew if I held the image of point B long enough, I would eventually move in that direction. I kept the faith and it worked. My advice is to focus on what you want, not what you do not want, to move out of resistance. Albert Einstein said, "We cannot solve our problems with the same thinking we used when we created them." I interpret this as the need to remove your resistance to items on your list to take action from responsibility. We can then take purposeful action without the weight of our negative thoughts.

Blaming is a common form of projection that creates resistance. It may sound like this: "He/She's the one that put us here." "It's not my fault." "She/he needs to have more interest in our finances." "If only she/he hadn't racked up all that debt." "If he/she would stop spending so much money." Part of taking responsibility for where you are is not reliving how or why you think things happened. Focusing on all the things you feel are to blame will surely keep them in your life and keep you from moving forward. The issue with blaming is your creativity to correct the situation is ng people, circumstances, etc., only causes you to lose creativity and your personal power.

Professional athletes understand this concept from the perspective of their sport. Let's say that a quarterback makes a terrible play that results in an interception. The play was a result of the quarterback temporarily losing focus and getting distracted. If the quarterback doesn't let go of this mistake, it is likely to happen again. He could get angry and say to himself, "That idiot! If only he didn't distract me, I could have made that play." As long as that thought pattern is going through his head, what do you think is likely to happen on the next play? They know they have to let bad plays go and focus on what they desire to happen.

When you are in a relationship, who is the easiest to blame? Your significant other, of course! It is usually easy for us to blame our partner for an undesirable financial reality than for us to take responsibility. This creates all kinds of negative energy on our partner, which in turn causes the situation to get worse. Years ago, my wife had quite a bit of bad energy on me and blamed me for the mess we were in. Although some of it was my fault, her continuing to resent me and have anger toward me was perpetuating our situation.

The best way to not blame each other and to begin the releasing process is through gratitude for your partner. Begin by thinking about all the things you love about him or her and why you are together. Write these down and continually update the list. If the negativity returns (we are only human and it usually does), go back to your list, listen to your thoughts, and shift to gratitude. The gratitude for your partner will help you to reverse the effect of the negativity and come from a perspective that will be open to create change.

Action Steps:

1. *Make a list of characteristics you see in others that irritate or annoy you in regards to money. How do you see this in yourself? Where and when did you learn to despise this characteristic? How does this affect your relationship?*

2. *Make a list of financial aspects in your life you wish were different.*

3. *What are some possible solutions?*

4. *Make a list of characteristics of your partner for which you are grateful.*

9.
Letting Go

Rule number one: If you create negative thoughts about your partner, you must find a way to stop. Harboring bad thoughts toward your partner is the quickest way to drive money away.

I shared the story earlier how I was resentful toward my husband. I experienced firsthand how letting go of resentment created positive change in my financial life. In talking with numerous financially independent couples, they have validated this principle. I have talked to financially independent couples who have never experienced resentment, even in times when most people would. I have met other financially independent couples who have gone through periods feeling resentment and learned to let go. As a result, they saw their financial situation improve, as I did. An example of this came from a friend who told me years ago she was resentful for all the money her husband spent on his business. She took a step back and realized she should be grateful for how hard her husband was working to provide a better life for them. Ironically, her husband was always the saver, and she was the spender. She knew she had to trust in his judgment, as she saw he was not making foolish financial decisions. This was a huge shift in their relationship and their financial life.

I was talking to another good friend about this revelation. This is the story of the controller/supporter combination that actually works. He is a successful entrepreneur and married to a wonderful woman he dated and lived with for almost five years prior to getting married. I have never seen him so happy! She is one of the most loving people I have ever met. She is grounded, grateful, giving, full of life, beautiful, and fun to be around. He is the main breadwinner supporting her and her two children from a previous marriage. She is somewhat indifferent about money and personally makes much less than her husband, but loves her work, which focuses on caring for people. She is a classic supporter. You may look at this situation and think this would be difficult for anyone to take on this type of financial burden. I asked him how that worked for him, as it really didn't seem to bother him. What he told me was one of the most romantic things I have ever heard. He said he saw so much value in having her in his life that the financial aspect doesn't faze him. He sees her as the yin and him as the yang, and being married to his wife brings a balance and completeness that he wasn't sure he could ever find. He thinks nothing of financially taking care of her because he sees her as an invaluable piece in his life. He feels it is a small price to pay and gladly accepts the financial responsibility. This is a great example of acceptance. There is no resentment or animosity between the two of them, and I believe his business continues to flourish because of this.

I have another great example of acceptance in a relationship that works. This couple has been married for fifteen years. The wife is currently the breadwinner; however, the husband has created wealth as well and is an entrepreneur. There have been high highs and low lows, yet the wife continues to keep her job and steady income. For some couples, this would put a huge strain on their relationship.

In talking with him, he realizes how hard his wife works and the prices she pays for him to be an entrepreneur. He is giving, kind, and always steps in to help out. He even stepped in to finish a major repair job when the contractor vanished and left a huge mess in their house. She was relieved when her husband stepped up, and she didn't have to worry about how it was going to get done. He works tirelessly toward his business success because of his desire to make up for the years of lost income and to relieve her of the financial burden.

She is okay with him being an entrepreneur and knows he works hard and wants her to have a better life. Her father was an entrepreneur and made a great living after years of struggling. She is in complete acceptance, and that is why they will do well financially long term and their marriage is strong.

One of the best ways I found to let go of resentment was to have fun. My husband and I turned saving money in to a game. We have a jar that we use to collect change.

This is not our main source of savings; however, we use it as a visual reminder in our house. We call it the Felton Financial Freedom Jar and were inspired to do this after reading T. Harv Eker's book *Secrets of the Millionaire Mind.*[2] We celebrate every new discovery of found money, even a penny found in the parking lot and add it to the Felton Financial Freedom Jar and hear it clank on top of the other coins. We call each other to announce that we just found gas five cents cheaper per gallon. All of these little wins create momentum for much bigger wins. It wasn't long before my husband and I were getting $500 and then $2,500 of unexpected money. If you don't believe me, focus on this game every day for at least a month and see what happens. My husband and I both have a hundred dollar bill in our wallets. We learned of this game from Jerry and Esther Hicks in *Ask and It Is Given.*[3] We have a hundred dollar bill in our wallet, so throughout the day we are "mentally" spending it. Instead of looking at something and thinking "I shouldn't" or "I can't," you are saying, "I could if I wanted to." This is one of the most powerful games I know of that helps to shift your attitude about money.

Be grateful! Every night my husband and I discuss what we are grateful for and good things that happened that day. Even a perceived "bad day" has parts that are good. If you got a parking ticket, were late to work, blah, blah, blah, blah, but the weather was great that day, there you go—that was something to be grateful for! We are grateful for every sign of abundance we can come up with—an empty parking space right in front, a bill that was less than expected. Being grateful causes you to look for evidence of positive events in your life instead of negative and to be on the lookout for more positive events. When you are looking for positive events, you will be more aware and open to these opportunities as they present themselves.

HIS PERSPECTIVE

One of the concepts I found to be very powerful is acceptance. This means accepting your current financial reality and taking responsibility. You cannot move forward until you accept responsibility. Personally, I had to acknowledge that I was stuck and how I got there. I could then move forward by removing resistance.

When you are in resistance, you feel stuck and experience denial and delusion. When you are in this state of mind, it keeps you from being open or even looking for possible solutions. I was there. I was in denial about where we were and delusional that it was going to get better. I just kept telling Marlow, "I am positive it's changing! I feel it." Being positive is important, but I was counting on outside circumstances to change our situation. So here I was, telling my wife things were going to change, but I was not changing and was continuing to do the same things over and over again, expecting a different result.

Easier said than done, of course. So you are probably wondering how you would do this. What I had to do first was to identify it. Resistance often takes on the form of worry, fear, blame, resentment, and anger. These are easy to identify because they usually cause a lot of emotion that consumes our thoughts. They are the items you wrote down from the chapter on resistance and projection earlier in the book. The best question to ask yourself is "How can I let this go?" I made lists of all the different ways I could let it go and/or deal with it. I created a list of free-flowing thoughts regardless of how absurd they sounded. I then asked myself: "What if this would work, and who could support me in making this happen?"

An example of this was a time I felt frustrated about our office space. It was a space that was more than we needed and costly. The more I thought about it, the angrier I got. Every month when the lease payment was due, there was more angst. I knew I had to let this go even if it was not possible to deal with it right away. I first took responsibility for my role in making it happen, even though I could have blamed others. I could have thought it through more at the time and consulted with others that I trust (my wife for one), but I didn't.

I then went to work on my list of possible solutions and had my wife come up with a list as well. We took this list and narrowed it down to the solutions that had the most potential to work out. We then consulted with our coach, a commercial realtor, and an attorney. The issues did not go away overnight; however, things started to improve with some smaller fixes of increased rental income to the office and some other short-term items we were able to negotiate. By seeing some movement in the right direction and feeling more in control of the situation, the resistance started to decrease. After over a year of working on this, we are close to a new permanent solution, and the resistance has significantly decreased.

People often ask me, "Where do we start?" Start from where you are, meaning point A. Most often people tend to focus on point B or other people's point A. This can cause a dangerous game of comparison of "keeping up with the Joneses," which can create big financial problems. It also feeds "We should not be here" thoughts, which is a form of denial. The reason people never move is they keep telling the same old story of, "We should not be here," or "We don't have enough money," which keeps you where you are, not having enough money. You cannot get to point B without knowing where point A is and accepting point A. If you live in Denver and want to go to Aspen, to get adequate directions, you have to type in the address of both point A (where you are) and point B (where you want to go). Too often, couples never define point A (where they are) together or take responsibility as an individual.

Have a meeting with your partner, define point A without blaming or justifying, and get it all laid out. This is powerful. I once did this for a client who was in debt up to his eyeballs. He had all his credit card statements buried in the kitchen drawer. He was obviously in denial. With interest rates that averaged around twenty nine percent, his wife was upset that he was hiding the situation. She calmed, and we defined point A by listing the debts and rates. Then he went into solution mode and was debt free in six months, just by defining point A. This also made him aware that it was not as bad as he thought and there was relief. He had created a bigger story than the reality, and his denial was only making things worse. Also, the fact that he hid this from his wife was more painful emotionally to her than the actual credit card debt. Creating a solution around it together was an important step in their marriage, and now that it is gone, the debt is not creating a silent emotional drag on their relationship.

Marlow and I did the same. We had the infamous "Come to Marlow Meeting," whereby our point A was defined. For me, being a positive person, I was taking an optimistic approach to the situation to our detriment. Unlike my client I just referred to, I made the situation less than it really was in my mind. The meeting was not pleasant, but it was necessary for me to see how I was being. I also had no idea how my denial was affecting my wife, and she made it clear how it was affecting her when she saw the reality. She had no idea the real situation I had created until AFTER we were married. The honeymoon was officially over!

Once I accepted where we were, identified point A, and took responsibility for putting us there, things started to change. I felt more in control and therefore took more focused action. What I mean is action that will produce the greatest results right now. I constantly remind myself of a phone call when my coach said, "What are you going to do right now when we end this call to turn things around?" I planted in my head, "DO IT NOW, DO IT NOW." I know of people who stated something as simple as "Do it now" created the greatest results in their life, and I can attest. I also thought about the action that would produce the greatest results. This was calling a prospective client vs. checking e-mail. Even if it was a small act, I knew it was a step in the right direction, and with every step, we were closer to our goal. Marlow and I constantly encouraged each other to do things now if the other is procrastinating on necessary action steps. Accountability and awareness served us well.

Action Steps:

1. *Write down issues you could have more acceptance to and possible solutions. How can you begin to let go?*

2. *Create ways to make saving money fun with your partner.*

3. *What are some actions steps you can "do now"?*

10.
Respecting Money

One of the most commonly overlooked concepts around money is respect, yet it is one of the most important. It is a reoccurring theme I see among financially independent couples. They respect money and money respects them. They respect their money and other people's money because they realize how they treat others' money is a reflection of their wealth. They also have a deep level of respect for their partner's money and need to have money for things important to them.

I have seen numerous examples of people that are broke disrespecting money. They will be the first to say, "It's only twenty dollars." Would you say, "It's only my wife"? They do not have a respectful relationship established with money. I see many people take advantage of wealthy people and their generosity. The people who are the first to order another drink when they find out someone else is buying or don't pay a financial obligation because they feel the person they are in debt to has plenty of money. I don't need to look at their bank account to know these people are broke. A wealthy person would not be disrespectful to someone else's money. People who are broke disrespect their own money as well. They are careless with relatively "small" amounts of money, which turn into large amounts. They will "throw away" seemingly small amounts of money over and over on things like extra large coffee drinks, sodas, cigarettes, vending machines, while they owe others money. Have you ever been in an apartment where someone has just been evicted? Yes, it is usually a mess because there was no respect for someone else's property, but there is something else that is interesting. There is usually a lot of change left behind. You can open drawers and find pennies, dimes, nickels, and even quarters. Sometimes the change is out in plain sight, lying on the floor. Someone had such little respect for money they wouldn't even bother to pick up a dime left on the floor, yet they can't seem to pay their rent. This is not a coincidence.

Many people believe wealthy people just mindlessly spend money. Well, some of them that may not hold on to their wealth do; however, financially independent people I know who have been this way for decades make respectful and strategic financial decisions. They respect money, so they would not go out and make a large purchase without making sure they were getting the best price and discussing it with their partner. They respect their partner's needs and will make sure they are respecting their money, their partner's money, and their financial goals.

HIS PERSPECTIVE

The topic of respect was a major awakening for me. I started to take money coming in for granted and wasted it when it arrived. I was frivolously spending on a daily basis unconsciously. It started adding up and created increased stress. What a paradox to experience financial stress, yet waste $25 plus per day without even realizing it. I justified the spending as small insignificant amounts. I now know I was being disrespectful to money.

As I began to study wealth and the related rules that govern it, I realized I had to respect all amounts of money no matter how small. My financial situation wouldn't stand a chance of improving until I did. I became a conscious spender, grateful for every dime and spent money strategically instead of haphazardly and paying myself first. I increased respect for my money, my wife's money, and other people's money, and money began to respect me. This may seem small and insignificant, but I have seen example after example proving the power of this concept. People who respect money are wealthy or on their way there, but people who disrespect their money or others' money are far from being financially independent.

Action Steps:

1. *Write down ways you have been disrespectful with your money or other people's money.*

2. *Write down ways you have been respectful of money. Think of how you can be more respectful to money.*

3. *Look for examples of wealthy people respecting money.*

11.

Segregating Funds: Theirs, Mine, and Ours

HER PERSPECTIVE

Being married for the first time at age thirty-nine, I spent the majority of my adult life financially responsible for only myself. Sharing money was a new concept for me, and I see it as a struggle for most couples. Some view the money they personally make as their money and vice versa. Whether a couple sees it this way or not, when you said, "I do," you also became legally financially linked. Where to put the money and how to budget can be a huge obstacle. People sometimes tell me they refuse to comingle any accounts for any reason and want to keep everything separate. I have met other couples that have only one checking account. They just do it that way because that's the way they think they are supposed to do it.

Let's take a look at why both of these situations might not work. The first displays a lack of trust and shows that a couple is not "on the same page" financially. Almost every time I have met with a couple who handles their money separately, I see other things that are not working in their relationship or their financial life. A good friend that is financially independent and happily married for over thirty years believes a marriage that does not have enough continuity and trust to share finances would not last. He saw example after example of this throughout his thirty-year business career. I know there are exceptions, but based on what I have seen, I would agree. I have seen couples stay together under these circumstances, but with some level of strain on their relationship.

The second example is the couple that shares one checking account and has only one checking account. This couple may be madly in love; however, they are in the delusional danger zone. Financial accountability and budgeting is difficult to manage with this system. I refer to this as the "checking account black hole." The couple sees the money in the account and uses it to buy whatever they feel they "need" at that time. There is always something to buy, so it always seems to disappear until the next paycheck, and the cycle starts again. Savings for retirement or short-term savings to buy a new home, car, etc., are ignored. These couples are the most likely to say they don't have any money to save.

Segregation of money is the easiest way to ensure priorities that require money like retirement, a new car, a new home, college, etc., will be funded. When seeing money in their checking account, people think nothing of heading out for dinner, as they don't connect the fact that they just took $50 away from their child's college education or their new home. A "black hole" checking account feeds the delusion that steals most couple's long-term dreams.

Several different systems exist for couples to segregate funds. Some have three checking accounts: Yours, Mine, and Ours. They have mutually agreed upon amounts of money that go into the "Ours" account each month and have agreed on what expenses will be paid out of this account. The key here is "mutually agreed upon." This is where compromise comes in. The "Yours" and "Mine" is the account for what is left. It is important that these categories be segregated as well in mutually agreed upon subcategories. I will diagram a few of these scenarios later in more detail.

A few years ago I came up with a segregated money category I named the "fun fund." The "fun fund" sounds fun, doesn't it? It was created from a particular experience that wasn't so fun. When first married, we both managed our own money. We were used to it and didn't know another way. Well, what ensued was a financial tug of war. We unknowingly were fueling a stressful situation and continuously committed financial infidelity! We used Chris's account for household bills and his personal expenses. I still had my personal checking account that I used for my bills and expenses. Since I was the saver, I also had a nice savings account I used for larger personal expenses and short-term needs. I had all my personal expenses, like getting my hair and nails done, and clothes strategically planned. It had worked great for me, until the day my husband had blown through his money, and suddenly we needed extra money to cover a large expense. Well, guess where the money had to come from? My savings account earmarked for a new suit. I was furious! How dare he take money away that I had earmarked for my personal indulgences? Does he not want me to look nice or be able to have a little fun every once in a while?

This started a downward spiral of resentment. I became aware of every dollar he spent. Every time he went to play golf I got an anxiety attack. How much money was he going to spend? Was he even aware of the nonexistent budget? Then I started to hide my purchases. I would go to the mall for a new pair of shoes and keep them in the trunk until he wasn't at home or was in the shower. Then I would sneak them up to the closet and get rid of the shopping bag evidence. I certainly didn't want him to think I was mindlessly spending money and encourage him.

I felt guilty every time I would do something for myself and try to hide it from him. I felt I deserved it; however, I was afraid of the negative impact it could have on his spending. There was also resentment when I wanted something and the money was not there. Then there is revenge spending, which is a great way to not save more money. Have you ever bought something for yourself just because your partner just spent too much on something without discussing it with you?

After years of minor financial infidelities between us, I thought there must be a better way. One day it hit me that what we really needed was some segregation and accountability for our finances. My husband really wanted me to be able to do things for myself. We needed some awareness, communication and an accountability system.

This was the inspiration for what I now fondly call the "fun fund." We would each have a "fun fund" we could use at our own discretion. We also had to agree on the financial categories it was to be used for. We agreed that if I wanted to get my hair done, nails done, a new outfit, a trip, etc., that was what it was for. If my husband wanted a new suit, to play golf, go out for a beer with the guys, or take a trip, his "fun fund" was there for him. We also agreed to include gifts to each other and to others.

I calculated our fixed monthly expenses and monthly savings. Based on this, we determined what amount per month would go in to our respective "fun" accounts. Yes, it would be the same for each of us. As we made more money and/or cut other expenses, we would be able to increase our monthly amount into the "fun funds."

I had no idea how my husband was going to react to this idea when I first discussed it with him. I mentally prepared for the delivery of my new idea, went downstairs, joined him on the couch, and proceeded to explain why and how I thought this was a good idea. There was a long pause as I waited for an answer. He then said, "That's brilliant." That's of course what I thought! We were on a new journey toward a successful financial marriage.

This may seem simple, but it has been one of the most important changes we have made to manage our expenses together. We discovered we spend less on these items and have more money for fun. It also removed guilt from our personal purchases and resentment on each other. I have talked to many couples who love this concept, and I have seen variations that work as well. Some refer to this concept as the "Yours, Mine, and Ours" accounts. The key is clearly communicated and mutually agreed upon uses and funding for these accounts, segregation, accountability, and the ability to have guilt-free fun with some money we can clearly call our own.

HIS PERSPECTIVE

Some people believe if they cut back on spending, it dramatically and negatively impacts their life. It was a story that I repeated for decades. The thought of cutting back for me was viewed as negative and created more spending. I also felt that it had to be dramatic and immediate. This didn't sound like much fun to me, and I know it doesn't sound like fun to most people.

If your goal is to climb a mountain and you are standing at the base looking at the top, it seems overwhelming and might cause most people to not get started. The key is to take the first step. The journey of a thousand miles begins with the first step. When cutting back, take small steps and eventually the momentum creates something magical. The reality is when you get control of your finances and become more consciously aware of the results, you start seeing changes. It may start off small; however, it will lead to long-lasting change. That is why it is necessary to take the first step and not get caught up in all the others before taking the first one.

People usually spend what they make unless they allocate their money correctly. It does not matter how much you have, you have to create "buckets" for where the money is going. We will talk more about "buckets" for saving, giving, education, etc., but one "bucket" that most people forget about is the "fun bucket". While making financial changes, it is necessary to have fun. If you are just all about the discipline, discipline, discipline, eventually you may self-sabotage your success. We all have an inner need to enjoy life and can usually only hold to strict discipline for so long. We are only human! You also gain a glimpse of the experience of financial freedom. Marlow created a "fun fund" for each of us. Depending on our monthly discretionary income, she allocates a portion to each of us on a monthly basis that is designed for fun only. We have agreed on the amount and how we can use it.

When we started this, it reduced resistance in our marriage, and fortunately, I didn't feel guilty about playing golf. I knew that Marlow felt better about it too, which was important to me. No man wants to come home from playing golf to an angry wife because he spent too much money. I was thrilled when Marlow created this and relieved by such a simple solution.

Stress and resistance can be created when couples try to budget and set financial goals. They begin to cut back and then one of them spends unnecessarily. I like to compare this to a crash diet. Eventually someone in the relationship will spend, and when that is not in alignment with the goal, it creates a financial and emotional tug of war, where no one wins. The "fun fund" concept is crucial to create accountability and boundaries, but to also allow each other to have fun. The creation of the "fun fund" for hobbies, eating out, entertainment, or sports, allows you to have fun, without guilt or reprimand from your partner. We also realized we did not have to wait to have fun in the future; we could start having fun with our money right away. We learned that the journey to your goal takes focused effort, discipline, and awareness and can also be fun. If you are not having fun with it, start masterminding with your partner about how to increase the fun and happiness. Also, as your income increases, the amount allocated to the "fun fund" should as well.

Action Steps:

1. *Discuss and agree on the amount that will go into your "fun funds" each month and the types of purchases each "fun fund" covers.*

2. *Create a "fun fund" for each other.*

3. *Think of ways to have fun that are low cost or free. Enjoy the process and have fun!*

12.

Cash Flow

To provide examples of effective segregation and budgeting, I have two flow charts for those of you still wondering how this works. The concept of segregation is powerful; however, there isn't one right way and many variations can be effective. I will explain a system of segregation that has worked well for us. The key is to communicate your feelings and thoughts so you can come to an agreement. You may need to tweak this as you discover what works and what doesn't.

First, think of your money as water being poured into a bucket. If you have just one bucket and your money is all being poured into it, you see the bucket is full. When you see the bucket is full, it is easy to see the water (money) and use all the water or spend the whole bucket. Why not? It's there. When seeing the bucket is full, spending on things that really aren't important becomes easy. Creating buckets for categories we want money for is important. Many couples use one account for all money coming in, so they don't realize when they are stealing from other areas of importance or fun. They would tell you there are other things they would like to have money for; however, they are unconsciously taking from those nonexistent buckets. Because they didn't create a bucket for those things or separate any money from the main bucket, they use everything in the one bucket and wonder why there never seems to be money for other things.

I recommend starting with one or two additional buckets. The buckets represent an account at a financial institution like a checking, savings, or other investment account. Please consult with a financial professional regarding these accounts. Short-term savings would be money needed in less than five years and could include major repairs for a house or car, emergencies, or a special trip. Mid-term savings is money intended for five to ten years and could include purchasing a new car, a new house, college education, or vacation home. Long-term savings is generally considered ten years or more. I refer to the short-term, mid-term, and long-term money as financial independence money. When these buckets are full and creating enough income on their own that requires no new money flowing in, financial independence has been created.

Household expenses are generally one bucket; however, depending on circumstances, you may want to add buckets to separate special household expenses. Children could be a bucket; Christmas or a family travel fund could be a separate bucket or subcategory of household expenses.

Keep in mind; although a travel fund of $1,000 a month might sound great, if that $1,000 a month is taking too much from the main bucket, there will not be enough for the other buckets, like short-term, mid-term, and long-term savings. However, maybe $500 a month might allow you to add to other buckets adequately, and then as the cash flow or income increases, the amounts for all the buckets can increase as well.

When you think of cash flow as water flowing into buckets, it allows you to visually segregate funds. When you do this, you see when there just isn't enough money coming in to adequately fill all the buckets, and the income must be increased. You also see when there is adequate money coming in and it is being siphoned off into the abyss of careless spending. When a bucket is created for an expense like a new home, you see the money accumulating for a down payment and can feel the excitement of accomplishing your goal. If you overspend in your household expense bucket and need to dip into the new home bucket, you can see the direct consequences of your overspending in the reduction of money for a new home. No matter how much or little you make, this concept helps you stay on track and accountable.

The following is a diagram of what I see most frequently. There is one main bucket where all the income comes into and out of. This is the cash flow diagram of the couple that says they do not have any money left over to save. They see it all in the bucket and continue to use that bucket without regard to other areas of their life, because those other buckets have not been created.

In the second example, all income is combined; however, other buckets or subcategories are created. The combined household income is used for combined expenses, savings, and giving buckets. The giving bucket is for donations to a charity or religious organization and an important aspect that cannot be ignored even if you have little money. Giving is an important part of receiving, and wealthy people understand this concept. The "fun fund" is then separated out for each partner. When other buckets are created in addition to the main household expense bucket, a couple can see when they are dipping into other areas of their financial life. They can also take a look at the household expenses, see where they may be spending unnecessary dollars, and then reallocate these dollars to another bucket that has not been properly funded. For example, I see couples that dine out frequently. They see they have money in their checking account, so they think nothing of spending the extra money. However, if they have a goal of buying a new home and have not set up a bucket for those dollars, they don't make the connection between the dinners out and their new home.

A variation of this could work for couples that have different core expenses because of children from a previous marriage, a separate business, or debts one partner is responsible for. These categories could be a subcategory of household expenses or separated from the main household expense bucket into a separate bucket. The flow into this bucket, however, would need to be mutually agreed upon.

I see variations of this example work. The key is to create the space for things that are important to you and segregate them in some way in order to be accountable. This does not mean you need twenty accounts for every category. Many couples can create an effective system with three to four accounts along with a few investment accounts for long-term savings. If you are just starting out, you might go from one account to three and include an investment account. Please talk to a trusted financial professional to determine what could work best for you. I would also recommend T. Harv Eker's jar system[4] (author of *Secrets of the Millionaire Mind*). If you are familiar with this and it works, please continue to use it. If you are not familiar with this system, please refer to the recomendations section in the back of this book. Segregating money is important, and whatever system works best for you is the one you should use. I have met many couples that say implementing a segregation system for their money changed their lives.

You may be wondering what to do if one partner makes significantly more income or one partner makes no income. The answer is: you do the same. The most successful couples see their finances as a partnership similar to a business. They both contribute in different ways, and the direct source of income is irrelevant. If they have agreed that one stay home to take care of the kids, that is his or her role in the partnership. If, however, the partner that is working is not bringing in enough money to fulfill the family's goals and dreams, a brainstorming meeting is in order. There must be enough cash flow to fill the buckets you have created and additional sources of income must be considered.

I know a couple that agreed to have one stay home with the kids only to find out after years of doing this, the partner creating the income had become resentful and stressed out from the responsibility, and the partner taking care of the kids felt insignificant. They didn't discuss this for years, as it silently affected their relationship. When I talked to them about creating buckets for areas of their life that were important to them, they realized they weren't making enough money. They made a list of possible income streams and discussed how they would work together to make it happen. They discovered a part-time business the partner taking care of the kids could do around the kids' schedule. The main breadwinner had to rearrange his schedule to help with some of the duties at home, but was happy to do so to help their overall situation. They have used the additional income to fund all their buckets and are on their way to financial independence, and the partner that once felt insignificant now feels a sense of contribution.

HIS PERSPECTIVE

The segregation of money is one of the best ways for couples to create a budget together. I have seen a variety of different systems that work. The common thread for a successful system is the mutually agreed upon buckets and accountability. Personally, it has made a huge difference for me and Marlow and has helped significantly to increase our cash flow and long-term savings.

If your cash flow is negative and/or you have a lot of debt, you still must create these buckets! Begin to put something in on a regular basis, no matter how small. It is critical that you begin the habit and fund these areas immediately. You should certainly pay off debt as well, but that should not be your only focus. You have to pay yourself and fund your goals and dreams along the way. If you feel the progress of paying off debt and funding the buckets is too slow, an increase in cash flow is in order. Refer to the section in this book "Multiple Streams of Income: Being Entrepreneurial."

Action Steps:

1. Make a list of financial "buckets" that are important to you.

2. Discuss with your partner possible "bucket" systems that can work for both of you.

3. Create at least one new "bucket" now and add something every week.

13.

Making the Shift

Do you feel stuck financially? The first step to get unstuck is to accept that feeling and define reality. Something had to change when I was feeling resentful and angry at my husband. There is great power in admitting you are stuck, but this doesn't mean you have to inform friends and family you are drowning in credit card debt. I do NOT recommend that. You should openly discuss where you are together and confide in someone you trust for help no matter your current level of success or the size of your ego.

When I say there is power in acceptance, I am speaking from experience. Once we took inventory of our situation, talked about it, and shared it with our business coach, we saw a shift. We accounted for our spending down to the penny. We looked back over a year of expenses and were shocked. If not tracking your expenses, please don't wait until you have a year's worth of history to review. Instead of doing a hypothetical budget, you must create a budget based on reality. This is part of your point A. You have to

81

know where point A is to be able to get to point B, or your goal.

Next, we talked through where we were with our coach and came up with a ninety-day goal, an annual goal, and a five-year goal. It was liberating just to tell another human being the reality of the situation and that we deserved better. Choose this person carefully. He or she must be trustworthy and be where you would like to be financially. Our coach has been financially free for decades. We only take advice from those who have the results we want. Too many take advice from others without really looking at that person's results. We have consulted with other trusted friends in the financial services industry that are financially independent as well.

We then clearly defined our point B together, or our end goals. We started with a ninety-day savings goal, an annual savings goal, and a five-year savings goal. We discussed how this would change our life and what we would do with the savings. One of the annual goals was to buy a new house. We gained clarity about where this house would be and what it would look like. This may seem simple; however, saying "we want to save more money" doesn't work.

We also developed a list of things to do once we hit our savings goal. We wrote down places we would go, experiences we would share together, and how it would positively impact people's lives around us. We shared our dreams with each other. Every financially independent couple I have ever met could tell me their partner's goals and dreams. This is the fuel that feeds the fire of your income, savings, and your relationship. Having more money in your life is meaningless without dreams to fulfill and experiences to share.

Without attaching a purpose to increased income and savings, couples can get off course. A partner can steer the other off course by losing sight of their goals and dreams or point B. They can rationalize to each other about making a major purchase they shouldn't be making. The emotional involvement of the relationship feeds an illogical emotional decision (like sex), and when emotion is high, intelligence goes down. We made a couple of large purchases in a similar fashion. We both really wanted it, and neither one of us stopped the other. We just forged ahead hoping the other wouldn't come to their senses. We also gave gifts out of love that sabotaged our long-term goals and dreams because we weren't as clear as we are now.

I met with a lady who told me a story of her husband taking her out to dinner. She loves going out to dinner and enjoyed the evening at their favorite restaurant. The dinner soon turned to indigestion when she realized the thoughtful gesture from her husband had not been well thought out with their checkbook register. She discovered the next day the charge for the dinner as well as the overdraft charge. Men, this may be a good way to get lucky after dinner, but not a good way to create long-term marital bliss.

My husband took me on a nice trip for my birthday a few years ago. At the time, we had not merged our finances, and I was not aware of the financial implications of this trip. I thought it was sweet of him, and we had a great time; however, when I became aware of our financial reality, I would have rather not taken the trip or made it shorter. Paying for that trip kept us from doing other things that were more important to us. I feel my husband got emotionally blindsided by the desire to do something special for me and lost sight of what we both later agreed was more special—our financial independence!

HIS PERSPECTIVE

I will never forget the day I spoke with our coach about our situation. I said I didn't understand why we were in that situation. My coach said, "Chris, asking 'why' is one of the worst questions. All it does is justify why you are where you are and keeps you stuck." The best question to ask yourself is, how am I going to *be* different moving forward? Not just what are you going to *do* different, but how are you going to *be* different? This represents the inside work or the emotional work. What my coach meant was I was approaching our situation from a worried and scarce state of mind. As a result, I was getting more worry, scarcity, and undesirable results.

When faced with a challenge, "Why me?" is a dangerous question to ask. When you ask "why me," you put yourself in a passive role as a victim as if the situation is a result of outside forces that have nothing to do with you. Instead, ask yourself, "How can I learn and grow from this experience?" This new question can help you move from being a victim of your circumstances to being RESPONSIBLE. You can make change from a place of being responsible because if you got yourself there, you can get yourself out.

Being positive is good, but I crossed the line to denial and was not being real. (Optimism and denial are the closest of friends.) I thought continuing with my current solutions of just working more and making more money would eventually get us there. I was in denial and not willing to take a hard look at the results. My internal programming, adopted at a young age, was unconsciously running my life. I realized I was like most men and thought, "just give me a peanut butter sandwich, a dime, a sword a few dragons to fight, and I will be fine." Meaning, I do not need the security. I was fine with the way things were; however, having a woman in my life to love and build a life with WAS important. Maybe I wasn't concerned about financial security, but she certainly was! When I connected the dots of creating financial security to fulfill a need for my spouse, it hit me like a ton of bricks. "Being different" then took on a new meaning and became urgent.

Change occurred when I realized how I was being and how the lack of results affected my wife and my marriage. Most people do not make changes until they recognize the true cost and pain they have caused. This is powerful when we connect it to our loved ones. I certainly did not mean to cause pain for Marlow, and I wanted to give us the life we deserved, but I was allowing bad money habits to sabotage those results unintentionally.

I decided how I was going to *be* different. I knew our financial challenges were never going to stop until I became a different person. I thought about all the people I respect and how they act and react in different situations. What would they do? How would they be? What characteristics do they have? Gratitude? Excitement? Love? I thought about all of these characteristics and wrote them down.

I then constantly reminded myself (with that piece of paper) how I wanted to *be*.

Have you ever known people who go through a bankruptcy only to be back within years? How about all the countless stories of people winning the lottery and being broke within a decade. They never understood how to be different mentally. *Being* the same person who got you into an undesirable situation cannot *be* the same person who gets you out or KEEPS you out.

Wealth is created from the inside out, and it is important for couples to evolve together. Evolution of the person must occur to transform financial challenges. The financial challenges will always arise; however, how you deal with them can be different. This is what I call *being different*. I believe the financial challenges were ultimately blessings and tests for me to evolve. I look at it now as part of *being different* training. I don't believe Marlow and I would have the relationship we have today if it were not for working through these challenges together. When I've asked wealthy people about their challenges, they state taking those away would take away their success. They believe whatever the challenge or price they paid was worth it.

I realized I had to keep the faith it would work. Faith has been a key ingredient to happiness and success in my life, as there were times when it was tested and it appeared things were getting worse. I began to develop the mental strength to focus on what we wanted vs. what we did not want. I kept the faith in myself and Marlow and let her know I had faith in her to help her keep the faith as well.

Action Steps:

1. *Define your "point B" in as much detail as possible.*

2. *Set aside time every day to visualize your "point B."*

3. *List your compelling emotional reasons for achieving this goal.*

14.

Multiple Streams of Income: Being Entrepreneurial

We are entrepreneurs, so I am familiar with fluctuating income. It is not for everyone; however, I wouldn't have it any other way. The only thing that could possibly get in the way of my husband and I making more money is us. I had a revelation a few years ago when I was frustrated with the amount of money coming in. I felt it should be more based on the years of effort my husband and I had put into our business. Where is this money, and how can I get it to come in faster? It then occurred to me, the money wasn't going to just appear out of thin air. It was somewhere at that moment. All the money I needed to make my dreams come true was somewhere; I just had to find it. I had to be open to opportunities and create value for other people for this money to come to me. Think about it! People need products, services, and information and are willing to pay a fair price for it. I just had to get out of my own way and be open to possibilities and solutions.

Almost every financially independent couple we know is entrepreneurial and has created multiple streams of income. They want as many different sources of income flowing in to their "buckets" as possible since there is no guarantee that one will continue at a consistent level. I have seen many couples successfully create additional streams of income while keeping a full-time job. They found something they enjoyed doing that took very little of their time. I know many couples who attribute their numerous income streams for carrying them through the recent recession. They watched some income streams go away and were grateful to have others that were growing.

Chris and I talked about this concept and brainstormed about the value we could bring people. We agreed to brainstorm as many ideas as possible, no matter how ridiculous they sounded. We went through the list, focused on the ideas we felt were the best, and came up with several new ways to make money. They were ideas we could implement with little money and time utilizing our personal resources and network of friends. Some of these areas are still sources of income for us today, while others didn't work out. This book was one of our ideas. The key is to work all angles and all solutions.

Many couples just need to make more money. For some, financial bliss is only as far away as a huge injection of cash. You must, however, check your attitude toward your partner's ability to make money, to ensure it is temporary. As I discussed earlier, resentment will not help the situation.

Supportive action toward common goals and being open to opportunities to create multiple streams of income is critical. I have brainstormed with couples on ways they could make more money. It is amazing to me how people can focus on all the reasons ideas can't work as opposed to all the reasons it could. That is the best way to stay broke!

As you brainstorm together, write down everything even if it sounds silly. If you start coming up with excuses of why it won't work, ask yourself "if I were to take these excuses away, would I still want to do it?" Set the excuses aside and look at the possibilities without the excuses. Also, your partner may develop solutions you haven't thought of. Remember to stay solution oriented and avoid excuses.

I have met with a variety of couples, with a variety of career choices. There can be the "stay at home mom" or even the "stay at home dad." Does "stay at home" mean "can't create any income"? I have met some creative women with prosperous businesses that take little of their time. They are able to run their business, pick the kids up from school, get dinner on the table, and spend quality time with their kids. They did it because they were open to possibilities and their family is more financially stable because of it. They were able to do it through leveraging their time and efforts. By this, I mean utilizing resources available to be efficient with your time and maximize income. The successful entrepreneur uses leverage. I also believe that leverage begins with your partner. Who else should be more supportive and interested in your success?

A couple we know that is financially independent got that way by being entrepreneurial. Early in their marriage, the wife stated it was often difficult because they struggled financially. She was resentful of him in the early days when his business was not bringing in enough to pay their bills. She had to trust her husband and that he was working to give them a better life. She understood what his business could do for them long term, because they had discussed it in great detail and she was open to the possibilities. She even sold her car to cover expenses when the business could not.

Another couple we know has been successful as entrepreneurs and learned to work together and support one another as business partners. One of the most important things my husband and I have done was to learn from their example. It has helped us to see what it takes to have an ideal business. Having mentoring relationships like these has been invaluable to us. Who better to call when dealing with adversity or a big decision than someone that has successfully overcome the same challenges? If you don't have these people in your life, find them!

I remember having a conversation with the friend a few years ago who shared with me how she and her husband work together and compliment each other's strengths. They knew the areas of their business they liked and the areas they did not. They talked through these areas and decided to focus on the things they liked and let the other do some of the things they didn't like. It worked out that each liked what the other disliked. They also support each other by referring people to each other as the "expert" in that area of their business.

We increased our communication regarding our business and constantly brainstorm areas of priority. We consult with other financial and personal mentors to increase results.

HIS PERSPECTIVE

Many couples are a few paychecks away from financial collapse, and a cut in pay would create tremendous pressure. Gone are the days of working for a company for forty years and getting a pension and a gold watch. Baby boomers are seeing this as they hit their fifties and sixties. Corporations show them the door, and their lack of planning creates significant financial problems. The issue is others are watching this and still repeating this same behavior. People need a plan B, an entrepreneurial business they can build on a part-time basis or potentially full-time. This is what happened to me. I worked for a great company, but as I stood back and looked to people who were ten to fifteen years ahead of me, I asked myself, "Is that where I want to be?" The answer was no as I saw lack of time and control. I wanted to build my own balance sheet.

I went looking for a business, and the prospects were not encouraging. I realized 80 percent of small businesses fail in the first two years. Most small business owners do not have a system, which significantly increases risk and is why most fail. They also lack proper coaching and mentoring. I read numerous articles of financially free business owners, and the majority stated the #1 reason for their success was that someone who had already achieved success showed them the way.

You must have passion for a business. People sense passion and want to work with people who are passionate about what they do. It will also help to get you through the rough times. You must have high belief in the product/ solution you are offering. If you do not have belief, it will not work. Doing a business just for money will not sustain you. You have to be completely sold on the value your business brings to others. The money will flow when you are "in service" to others and are excited about the difference you can make. While searching for your business that meets these criteria, ensure the industry you are choosing has a large market with a tremendous need for your offering. Timing in business is crucial as well. I have watched talented people whose businesses did not make it because of bad timing. Mentoring could have helped avoid this.

Give your business time to grow as I have watched people look for instant gratification. Like a farmer planting their crop, you must be patient. A farmer wouldn't give up on his farm right before the crop begins to grow. This is one reason you may want to consider a part-time commitment to a new business. You must also have a personal development game plan to grow yourself in order to grow your business.

It is critical to have your partner's support as well. Whether you work together in the business or not, the income will benefit both of you, so you must be in agreement on the business, the time, and the resources required for it to work. I know couples who have worked together on a new business while maintaining their full-time employment to keep their cash flow consistent. Other couples have agreed to have one work full-time on the business, while the other holds a full-time job to support the cash flow and contributes to the business on a part-time basis. Discuss what works best for you and be in agreement with the long-term plan.

Action Steps:

1. *Have a mastermind session with your partner. Think of any and all ways you may have to create additional income.*

2. *Discuss the best ideas from that list you could start to implement right away.*

3. *Make a list of people who would support you.*

15.
Your Financial GPS System

When we saw things had shifted, it was like we had a financial GPS System on at all times. We knew where we were, where we wanted to go, and most importantly if we were on course. Most every action we do every minute of every day is either moving us closer to our goal or farther away. We think of every financial decision in that way no matter how small. If your goal is to save $20,000 for a down payment on a house, bringing lunch to work instead of going out to lunch (and actually saving the difference) is a small change, but over time the extra $5 a day of savings is $100 a month or $1,200 a year, which brings you closer to your goal. Choosing to go out to lunch and not save the money takes you farther away.

A financially independent friend explained that early in his marriage when he was in his early twenties he made the connection between saving small amounts of money every day and what that would mean for his family decades later. When he looked at a dollar, he didn't see just a dollar, he saw what it could mean for his family in the future if he was willing to set it aside and NOT spend it. Where do you waste $3 each day? Three dollars a day is $100 a month. If you earn an 8 percent return on that $100 a month, in twenty years you will have $57,732. In thirty years, it would be $142,768. What would $142,768 mean for you if someone were to give you that money today? Are you willing to find $3 or more a day to turn a simple habit into financial independence?

Most people are struggling financially because they don't have enough money working for them. Having money working for you is building equity in your life. Most people diligently pay their bills every month, think nothing of paying $5 for a cup of coffee, spend $10 here, $20 there, as if it is no big deal. That money is going to work for someone else; why not have it work for you? This is known as "paying yourself first." The best way to show this is by explaining the rule of seventy-two. This is the law of compounding interest. If you take seventy-two and divide it by the rate of return earned, that is the number of years it takes for your money to double. The chart below shows what a one-time $10,000 investment will be at different rates of return from ages twenty-nine through sixty-five.

The difference between a 4 percent rate of return and a 12 percent rate of return is huge. Get advice about how this can work from a trusted financial professional and implement a strategy to minimize risk as well.

4% Rate of Return	6% Rate of Return	8% Rate of Return	12% Rate of Return
Doubles every 18yrs	Doubles every 12yrs.	Doubles every 9yrs.	Doubles every 6yrs.
Age 29 $10,000	Age 29 $10,000	Age 29 $10,000	Age 29 $10,000
Age 47 $20,000	Age 41 $20,000	Age 38 $20,000	Age 35 $20,000
Age 65 $40,000	Age 53 $40,000	Age 47 $40,000	Age 41 $40,000
	Age 65 $80,000	Age 56 $80,000	Age 47 $80,000
		Age 65 $160,000	Age 53 $160,000
			Age 59 $320,000
			Age 65 $640,000

If your partner is a spender, run numbers to show them the results of saving ten, twenty, or thirty years from now. Think about what your life would be as a result. Many couples that are financially independent started here. They both had a dream and then ran the numbers to see how it could happen. This is saving with a purpose. Saving doesn't always sound fun, but when a couple makes the emotional connection about their future quality of life, changes begin to happen easier. Spenders become focused savers.

Look at the earlier chart in regards to debt. Paying 12 percent on a credit card is having this work for someone else, not you! See how detrimental this can be when you spend hard-earned money toward interest on debt instead of it working for you? Financially free couples confirm being debt free is critical, yet struggling couples can't seem to pay off their credit cards. I believe it is because they never save any money and are never willing to lower their standard of living or do whatever it takes to make more money. What happens when they have no money saved and the car needs a $1,000 repair? They put it on a credit card, and once again, more money is working against them. Start the shift by saving even a small amount every month. It adds up and gets you in the habit. Financially independent couples we know said they consistently saved even when it hurt.

Another destructive pattern I see couples buying into is the tax refund illusion. They get excited about a huge tax refund. What do they usually do with that money? Pay off credit card debt. They spend the entire year paying the credit card company interest to borrow money, while loaning the government money interest free. They act as if this refund is "found" money when it was theirs to utilize throughout the year. The compounding consequences are substantial over time. Talk to a CPA about the steps needed to avoid this situation.

HIS PERSPECTIVE

I want to share with you a great exercise to do with your partner. We were introduced to this process by our good friend, Deron Ferrell. Below you will see a list of some financial goals that may be important to you and/ or your partner. I suggest completing this separately. Please place an X next to those goals that are important to you.

Retirement Savings____   College for Kids/Self___   Travel___

Own a Business____   Build Estate___   Charitable Contribution___

New Home___   Debt Free___   Short-Term Savings___

Support Aging Parents___   New Car___   Financial Independence___

On a scale of one to ten, ten being the most disappointed, how disappointed would you be if you did not hit those goals? If the potential disappointment is less than a five, you are not serious and should get clear on a goal that is emotional for you. If five or greater, let's continue and see how serious you are. Now compare with your partner.

The next test will measure your level of commitment by assessing accountability for your spending. Each of you can answer these questions and record below. From the time you wake up, go to work, and come back home, think about everything you spend money on (coffee, bagel, lunch, bottled water, trip to the vending machine, food at the gas station). Add these up for both of you. How much was it? Now do the same for the evenings. How many trips to eat out? Entertainment? Add this up. How about the weekends? What is the total spent on a weekly and monthly basis?

Daily Spend: ____   Per Week: ____   Per Month: ____

Nightly Spend: ____   Per Week: ____   Per Month: ____

Weekend Spend: ____   Per Week: ____   Per Month: ____

Total Spend Per Month: ____

New Savings Per Month Commitment: ____

Would you say these dollars you are unconsciously spending are not helping you achieve the goals noted above? You stated you were serious about hitting these goals, correct? With these wasted dollars, what if you took 50 percent and put it toward these important goals? Take the weekly spend, find a financial calculator use an interest rate of 5 to 8 percent, and project what this could mean for you and your family in five years, ten years, or twenty years.

People often say they do not have any money to save. It is amazing to see the value of unconscious spending when they go through this process and see they really do have money to save. We know a gentleman who blew $25 per day unconsciously. That's over $9K per year. Earning 5 percent interest over just ten years equates to $135,376. Wow! He was totally unconscious about it and believed this small amount wouldn't make a big difference. Obviously it does. I shutter to think of the money I have blown in the past when a small shift in consciousness could have saved me a fortune.

This exercise is important to do with your partner so you can hold each other accountable. This will also help to refocus your awareness on your goals and dreams. You work hard for your money, so don't let these little slips impact your future.

Action Steps:

1. *Define your most important financial goals and share with your partner. Determine the cost to achieve these goals.*

2. *Spend the next few days discovering wasted money. Find your weekly, monthly, and yearly amount. Find a financial calculator and calculate what this could be in five, ten, or twenty years.*

3. *Discuss with your partner how you can begin today putting these wasted dollars to work for you.*

4. *If you have debt, look at the interest you are paying and discuss how you can put these wasted dollars to work eliminating debt.*

16.
Financial Intimacy

Financial intimacy is when a relationship is free of financial resistance and a couple has complete trust and financial continuity. They have achieved a level of intimacy that creates a harmonious lifetime bond. Characteristics of couples who have reached a high level of financial intimacy are as follows:

They let go of past financial relationships with others or themselves. For me, it was my financial relationship with myself and those bad financial decisions I was projecting on Chris. I had to let that go. For others, it's the need to let go of past financially dysfunctional relationships. If a former partner was a frivolous spender, that does not mean a new partner will be a spender. I have seen partners freak out when the other spends money that seems frivolous because it brings back the fear and pain of a past partner. Often they are unaware of why they are reacting this way.

Let's compare this concept to sexual infidelity. If someone has previously been cheated on, often they bring that fear into a new relationship. How would people act if they are fearful someone may cheat on them? They might be overly nosey or clingy with the new person. Does this ever help a relationship? Dealing with that fear and communicating it to the new partner is an important step toward creating intimacy in the new relationship. The same is true with our financial relationships. When two people have no guards up and do not let negative financial baggage get in the way, they are open to complete trust that produces a powerful force. This financial bond can catapult a couple to increased financial levels over and above what they would do independently. They are open to more financial possibilities and work much better as a team to create income.

Imagine a trapeze artist leaping toward the oncoming bar without letting go of the one they are on. It requires commitment to let go of one bar to grab the oncoming bar. Much is gained when we allow ourselves to completely trust. We emotionally put ourselves at risk; however, the result is a huge reward of intimacy and financial harmony.

Complete trust is difficult, and I know many couples on a second or third marriage where complete trust becomes understandably difficult. It may take time for even a perfectly matched couple. There are other couples where there is little trust and it is clear why. I often wonder the motivation for them to get married in the first place.

HIS PERSPECTIVE

In my previous marriage, I thought I had to do everything and make financial decisions without any accountability to my spouse. As a result, it created negative results. There was a lack of financial harmony. Being with Marlow, I brought my past financial behavior and beliefs with me. I didn't realize I was bringing old behavior that never worked into this new relationship and expecting a different result. Similar situations and issues were recreated. I had to let go of my old beliefs and related bad emotions, start out with a clean slate, and open myself up to accountability.

I felt the shift when we came together and wrote down some financial goals we agreed on. We each had several goals; however, we both felt the most important was saving money. This became our number one financial thought, which ended up spilling over to other areas of our lives not only financially but emotionally. We began to make more money, and our relationship grew.

We created a mastermind. My definition of a mastermind is when like-minded people come together for a common goal and utilize the knowledge of all the members collectively. What usually happens when the group is in alignment is the results created are infinitely greater than any individual could create alone. When you create a mastermind with your partner, it becomes a powerful force creating bigger results and incredible intimacy. The results can be more than twice as powerful, but infinitely more powerful. When a couple is on the same page romantically, emotionally, and financially, synergy and velocity is created.

16. Financial Intimacy

Action Steps:

1. Discuss with your partner your single most important financial goal.

17.
Being on the Same Page

How do you get on the same page? As one couple told me, it is important for couples to see things the same way and ensure everything they do is consistent with that vision. They see everything they do as either putting them closer to their dream or farther away. He sold her a dream of how they would be able to live if certain financial goals were met. If they didn't take action to change their results, they would continue down the same path they didn't want. They worked toward this common vision for their future with every financial step they took and were accountable to each other.

We often react to an action from a partner, which is a symptom. To get on the same page with your partner, you must discover the root of that symptom. Spending is not a root cause as saving is not a root cause. Having a need for approval, feeling unworthy, and fear are root causes. A male friend married to a spender realized just saying something or trying to compensate for a partner's symptoms doesn't change her. He spent many years trying to cover up his wife's spending (which was a symptom) with just making more money and found it didn't work. The spender wife realized she was spending to show love. She is a classic supporter and needs to show and receive love. This was the root cause of her behavior. When she realized what she was doing and thought about what this could be teaching her kids, she stopped. She didn't want to teach them self-destructive financial habits.

The husband being a saver thinks, "Is that a want or a need?" Waste is all the little things that add up. Discipline and the thrill of knowing that he could, have saved him millions of dollars over the years. He has a six-month rule for all large purchases. If he wants something, he waits for six months to buy it even though he has the money. He has found many times after the six months has passed, he doesn't want it anymore. Have you ever heard the saying, "Fantasy is better than reality"? This applies to money too. Delaying gratification can cause you not to purchase something you thought you needed. You may be able to afford it, but you can bask in the glory of knowing you could and realize one day you really don't need it after the thrill of the moment is over. A number of financially independent couples I know use this technique.

This spender/saver couple got on the same page and decided to agree on every expenditure. He created two sides of their financial partnership—a business budget account and a home budget account. He was in charge of the business account, and she was in charge of the home account. The house account was given a mutually agreed upon annual income, and the wife budgeted all home expenses for herself and the kids. If she spent all the money in the house account, she could not go to the business account for more funds. He forced their savings on a monthly basis through the business, since he knew she was the spender. Income went into the business account, and then twice a month, the business wrote a check to the house account that was a joint account. They stuck to their budget, segregated the funds to the appropriate account, and never borrowed or comingled no matter what! This couple has been married for over thirty years and has been financially independent for the majority of that time. They believe couples that last see the money as "theirs." They see their financial life as a partnership and trust the other is doing his or her job.

Financially independent couples always maintain a consistent, disciplined savings plan. One referred to it as the lifeblood to their long-term financial stability. They save even when it hurts. They know saving money and keeping money saved is imperative. I have watched many couples make a great deal of money but never save. Some save small amounts at a time only to take the money out because their standard of living is beyond their current means, thus sabotaging their long-term goals and dreams.

The best way I have heard this explained was by a friend who is financially independent. He said there are only three main parts to our financial life: (1) income, (2) spending/living expenses, and (3) savings. He knows saving is critical to long-term financial stability, and his goal was to grow their savings to create enough income to live on.

Most couples lack the discipline to consistently fund savings with their income, or they lack the discipline to live below their means to save. My friend told me: you have to be willing to let some things bleed in order to save the piece that is the most important (the savings). He refers to savings as the main artery of financial independence. It might get bloody at times to keep the savings going; however, without it, financial independence will never happen. There are couples who consistently save for a period of time to grow the savings to live on, only to raise their standard of living and erode their savings. It may seem illogical, but this is what happens to most. Emotions get the best of many, and they forgo the discipline that got them where they are. My friend told me they always remember the discipline that got them there, and that is what keeps them there.

HIS PERSPECTIVE

People often get overwhelmed with lofty goals, and we were no exception. What we did was chunk down the goal. This means to break down a big goal into a series of smaller goals in a shorter period of time that feels achievable. In the past, I would get close to my deadline and realize how much needed to happen. Feeling overwhelmed, I gave up and then reset the same goal further in the future.

Our coach taught us to set ninety-day goals that aligned with our annual goals. We had an annual savings goal, divided into quarterly goals. Then we broke it down further to a weekly goal and noted the actual steps required to hit our weekly goal. This became part of our weekly action plan. If a couple has an annual savings goal of $15,000 and they have never saved $15,000 in a year before, it can seem impossible. However, if focused on $288 a week or even $42 a day, it sounds much more attainable. If it seems more attainable, the couple is more likely to take action to achieve the goal.

For us, our savings goal was our number one priority. We chunked the goal down and knew what we had to do every single day to make the annual goal happen. We also tracked our progress together. This was extremely important. Imagine if we set the daily, weekly, and monthly savings goal and then never knew what actually happened? You can't climb a mountain by walking around in circles at the base.

The other key ingredient to setting goals is connecting it to compelling emotional reasons. For me, it was for Marlow to live her ideal life, free of financial stress, and live in a house she loved. We spent three years in a house my wife hated. I wanted her to be happy in a spacious home in a safe neighborhood where we could enjoy being outside and have fun together. I spent a lot of time thinking and visualizing how this would look and feel. This became our compelling emotional reason. We calculated the necessary savings needed to buy the home we wanted and worked together to make that a reality. We held each other accountable and created urgency. Because we were so connected to the emotional reasons, it became something we had to do, instead of just something we wanted to do. I believe our focus on one positive goal was an important key. People tend to focus on a negative item like getting rid of debt or have too many scattered goals, so they lose focus and none of the goals are met.

Couples are busy and so distracted they do not communicate short and long-term goals. Many couples don't even know the things that are important to each other. The urgency of everyday life causes couples to be unclear about where they want to go. Would you start out on a road trip to see a relative without finding out where he or she lived? Of course, not! However, many people live this way. People often make short-term decisions that jeopardize their long-term goals, dreams, and aspirations because they are unclear about what they want long term. Often the spender seeks instant gratification and makes impulse buys that move the couple off track. There are also clever justifications for the purchase. "You had a hard day" or "this was a special occasion" are popular justifications.

Lack of understanding about what the other wants causes one to think selfishly. Usually the selfish behavior is unconscious and habitual. When I became clear about what we wanted, I questioned these clever justifications for spending that did not serve us. When I developed the compelling reasons for wanting to save money and began to direct my thoughts toward this end, the emotion of it began to override the existing excuses for spending. When wanting to spend, the visual of us attaining our goal and my wife's happiness around this took precedence. It was my visual pop up or thought that I created to become conscious about the spending. I would sit back, close my eyes, and picture the ideal life that Marlow and I talked about. For fifteen minutes a day, I would close my office door, turn off the light, and picture in my mind Marlow and me on our dream vacation. I would let my mind wander with as much detail as possible, what I would feel, smell, taste, and hear. The best part was the feeling of joy that would come over me as I imagined the look on Marlow's face of sheer happiness.

Writing my compelling emotional reasons for what I wanted helped me to create the visual images. As I got better at visualizing, I began to reprogram my subconscious, do things differently as a result, and change began to happen. If you don't believe this will work, try doing it for fifteen minutes a day, every day, for at least twenty-eight days, and you will see positive changes. They may be small in the beginning, but the more you practice this, the momentum will increase. Our subconscious mind does not know the difference between a visual we create and reality. This is why visualizing with emotion and feeling is so effective when we want to reprogram our actions and, in turn, our reality.

Focusing on one major goal and getting crystal clear on the results can make a major difference in your life and relationships. In this busy world, it is easy to get distracted and lose focus. Sharing what you both want and knowing the other is counting on you to follow through is an important first step to getting on the same page. Accountability with your partner is necessary for you to remain on the same page. I took responsibility for my actions, got clear on what we wanted, held myself accountable to Marlow, and created lasting positive change.

Action Steps:

1. *Discuss with your partner goals that are most important to you and determine your common goal to focus on.*

2. *Discuss the steps required to reach this goal.*

3. *Break this down into an annual, monthly, weekly, and daily goal. Determine daily activity required to achieve this goal and be accountable to each other.*

4. *Visualize this end goal on a daily basis.*

18.
Celebrate

HER PERSPECTIVE

Celebrating is fun! When you are having fun, you have more value in your life. You must enjoy the process and make it fun by constantly celebrating. This is not a natural tendency for most people, so remind yourself to celebrate all wins no matter how small. When we started to celebrate more, we enjoyed the process more, and the more we enjoyed the process, the more progress we saw. Life is a journey and we can get bogged down in drudgery if we forget to celebrate.

HIS PERSPECTIVE

Looking back, one of the things that was the most fun and helped fuel action and results, was to celebrate all wins. It didn't matter how small; it was a step in the right direction. Marlow and I would call or text each other throughout the day if we found a penny or found a free parking space. Any compensation we would receive, we would celebrate. Obviously, we communicated bigger wins as well and gave thanks for the signs we were on the right path. This helped us stay excited and on track when our point B seemed far away. We knew without celebrating all wins, our energy and momentum would dissipate.

Most people only celebrate the major things in life, which creates a layover mentality, which means, celebrating the big moments and then suffering unconsciously through the moments in between. The reality is the time between the big wins that make up the majority of your life. You can choose to make these small wins more important and significantly impact the fulfillment of your life. Most people also collect evidence of all the things that are going wrong. A big part of making a shift toward what you want is to look for evidence you are moving in the right direction. Have you ever decided you wanted a new car? You saw an ad on TV and started dreaming about owning that car, and then you started seeing it everywhere you went. This is not a coincidence but goes to show you what happens when you shift your awareness to what you desire.

Marlow and I began to collect evidence that there was abundance in our lives. In the past, something good would happen, and I would mentally say, "Hey that is great, but I am so far from where I need to be." That sting of reality would cause me not to appreciate the moment and not to continue to look for more evidence of things going in the right direction, thus perpetuating the lack of the prosperity. This had to change, so every financial blessing of any size was celebrated. I would find a penny on the ground and call her and say, "Honey, guess what, we are money magnets. I just found a penny." Her response and excitement always matched mine and vice versa. My favorite phone calls were when she would call and say, "Guess what, I'm a money magnet…" and then tell the story of what happened. We began collecting evidence that things were changing, telling each other about the evidence, celebrating, and guess what? It began changing.

It was fun to look for evidence and then celebrate the change. Most people spend their lives always looking to the negative. Their view is "it is only a penny," and that is why they stay broke. We were always looking for ways to increase our cash flow and therefore more reasons to celebrate. To us, saving five cents a gallon on gas was bringing us that much closer to our goal and reason to celebrate! At the end of the day, while driving home, I always list out loud the things that went right that day. I have days when everything does not go right, so it is sometimes a challenge to find what went well, but I do. Even if it is as little as "Hey, my car started and worked." "I still have another day, another chance; millions do not have the opportunities I have." "I have a warm bed, and I never have to worry about food." This mentality of gratitude and celebrating will shift your world and provide continued blessings, as you will receive more instances and proof of abundance. When things go wrong, it is just a perception. Sometimes the so-called "bad stuff" is a delay for something better yet to come. A delay is not a denial.

Celebrating has increased our excitement, passion, bettered our health, relationships, and yes, our finances. To move forward financially as a couple, you must celebrate and look for evidence of prosperity every day to prove you are moving in the right direction.

18. Celebrate

Action Steps:

1. *Discuss with your partner small things you can celebrate on a daily basis.*

2. *Discuss some things that have already happened that you can celebrate.*

3. *Keep a daily gratitude journal.*

4. *Celebrate that you made it this far in the book! Celebrate if you had a conversation with your partner about this book! Celebrate if you did any of the action steps!*

19.

A Couple Whose Dreams Came True

I met with a couple a few years back, married twelve years, together for fourteen years. He was somewhat neutral with money but believed it was scarce based on his associations. His friends believed it was scarce, and their results proved this. His wife's dad told her to work hard to make money. Her dad thought rich people were crooks, so she grew up unconsciously believing this. As a result, this inhibited her ability to make money as she sabotaged her financial results, unconsciously. When hit with adversity, they discovered their old beliefs about money took over. When they were first married, she worked hard while the husband sat back and watched not knowing how or what to do. She was an avoider, so she neglected financial conversations with her husband. She wanted to know the money was there and that there was plenty of it. She wanted financial security the most.

Four years into their marriage, she hit rock bottom with fatigue and was forced to look for better career options.

The couple was going through a difficult time, reeling from a bad real estate deal that almost wiped them out financially. She was so distraught she could not get out of bed for three days. Her husband finally told her that no one could take away her happiness—only she was in control of her life. She began to feel in control, and they started to make changes together. They became open to all the possible solutions and focused on them as a team. When they realized they needed to let go of all the bad feelings they had toward the bad real estate deal and the feeling of being powerless to it, things began to change. Before long things worked out, and they found a solution that worked well. When I asked them what made the difference, they said their change of attitude toward it and their focused effort together.

They realized personal growth and knowledge was the key to growing their income, so they started attending seminars together. He understood he needed to change his associations and started looking for friends that were financially where he wanted to be and began reading books on the topic. She realized she needed to get clear on her ideal career, and she had to trust it would happen. She shared this dream with her husband (which was something she wouldn't have done in the past), wrote down the description of her ideal position, and read it out loud every day for thirty days. Amazingly, her dream career become a reality within a year and dramatically improved their financial situation.

This couple now implements a financial system that works for them. They are both controllers, share the financial responsibilities, and meet for an hour per week to go through their balance sheet. Implementing a system to segregate money has changed their life. They have an account for their mutually agreed upon expenses (similar to the outline shared in this book) and strategically allocate money for important items, including savings and fun. They hold each other accountable to stay within their limits, not overspend or dip into other areas. They treat their household like a company and review the balance sheet during their weekly meeting. They have separate incomes; however, they pool their incomes together first and then disburse funds according to their plan. This system not only helped create more money in their life, it has created more harmony in their relationship. He is an entrepreneur and investor, so he creatively looks for opportunities to create more freedom. He looks for investment opportunities to grow the balance sheet, which they discuss during their weekly financial session. If more urgent, a meeting is scheduled right away. They discuss the pros and cons, and if she is not comfortable with it, they don't proceed.

They are not without bumps in the road, but believe financial stress is only temporary and a choice. They believe financial setbacks do not control their happiness; they control their happiness. They got clear on what they wanted and stopped focusing on what they did not want. This has allowed them to stay solution focused when dealing with adversity. After dealing with financial adversity, they feel nothing can stop them and they can handle anything. They would tell a struggling couple to open their minds to doing things differently, grow together, stay as relaxed as possible, and be grateful for everything you have.

Summary of a Financially Harmonious Couple

1. They say and feel they are on the same page.
2. They have a mutually agreed upon financial segregation system that works for them.
3. They focus on what they want, communicate, and plan around it constantly.
4. The respect money, theirs, others, and each other's.
5. They feel that money is good, and they feel they deserve it.
6. They share a dream and are committed to creating that reality.
7. They utilize each other's strengths to work toward their goals together.
8. They have fun, yet take their finances seriously and treat household finances as a business.
9. They see the money as "Theirs" regardless of the direct source.
10. They hold each other accountable and maintain a positive attitude toward money.

11. They generously give to charitable organizations, and are giving of their time for the benefit of others.
12. They are open to multiple streams of income that can fund their goals and dreams.

Recommendations

Butterworth, Eric. *Spiritual Economics*. Unity Village, MO: Unity House, 1998.

Dyer, Wayne D. *The Power of Intention*. Carlsbad, CA: Hay House, 2004.

Eker, T. Harv. *Secrets of the Millionaire Mind*. New York: Harper Collins, 2005.

Ford, Debbie. *The Shadow Effect*. Directed by Scott Cervine. Debbie Ford Films and Hay House Inc., 2009.

Hansen, Mark Victor, and Robert Allen. *The One Minute Millionaire*. New York: Crown Publishing, 2009.

Hicks, Esther, and Jerry Hicks. *Ask and It Is Given*. Carlsbad, CA: Hay House, 2004.

Hicks, Esther, and Jerry Hicks. *Money, and the Law of Attraction*. Carlsbad, CA: Hay House, 2008.

Hill, Napoleon. *Think and Grow Rich Action Pack*. New York: Plume, 1990.

Holosync by Centerpointe. www.centerpointe.com.

Klemmer, Brian. *If How-To's Were Enough We Would All Be Skinny, Rich and Happy*. Tulsa, OK: Insight Publishing Group, 2005.

Manske, Jonathan. *The Law of Attraction Made Simple*. Parker, CO: Books to Believe In, 2008.

Millionaire Mind Intensive Seminar. www.millionairemind intensive.com.

Proctor, Bob. *You Were Born Rich*. Scottsdale, AZ: LifeSuccess Productions, 1997

PSI Seminars. www.psiseminars.com.

ReWrite Your Money Story. www.jonathanmanske.com.

Siebold, Steve. *How Rich People Think*. London House, 2010.

Taylor, Sandra Anne. *Quantum Success*. Carlsbad, CA: Hay House, 2006.

Tolle, Eckhart. *The New Earth*. New York: Plume, 2006.

Acknowledgments

Thank you to our wonderful family and friends. We appreciate the unconditional love and support that has inspired us to be who we are today. To Caden and Carson, you are a true source of inspiration for your dad and I love you.

To our incredible business team, we are deeply appreciative for all you have done for us. Your loyalty, hard work, dedication, perseverance, and support inspire us every day. Our success is because of people like you, and we are very grateful.

Thank you to our clients who have put their trust in us. We are grateful to be able to help you with something so important and value the relationships we have built over the years.

Thank you to Roy Dayton, your coaching, mentoring, and direction was significant to helping us. We are forever grateful.

A special thanks to Monte and Lisa Holm for your example and friendship. We are grateful for all you have done for us!

Acknowledgments

Thank you to Joe Gregory, Megan McDonald, Lorrie Tietze, and Deron Ferrell for their wonderful contributions to this book.

About the Authors

Marlow and Chris Felton live in Denver, Colorado. They have a combined nineteen years experience in the financial services industry working with couples of all walks of life. They are business partners and mentor over ninety financial professionals. They are students of personal development, which led to their financial transformation they share in *Couples Money*.

For more information—or to schedule a lecture or seminar visit us at www.couplesmoney.com.

Endnotes

[1] PSI Seminars. www.psiseminars.com.

[2] Eker, T. Harv. *Secrets of the Millionaire Mind*. New York: Harper Collins, 2005.

[3] Hicks, Esther, and Jerry Hicks. *Ask and It Is Given*. Carlsbad, CA: Hay House, 2004.

[4] Millionaire Mind Intensive Seminar. www.millionairemindintensive.com.

Made in the USA
San Bernardino, CA
05 April 2018